D1292505

Remaking Ibieca

Remaking Ibieca
Rural Life in Aragon
under Franco

Susan Friend Harding

University of North Carolina Press

Chapel Hill and London

© 1984 The University of North Carolina Press

All rights reserved

Manufactured in the United States of America

Library of Congress Cataloging in Publication Data

Harding, Susan Friend.
  Remaking Ibieca.

  Bibliography: p.
  Includes index.
  1. Land reform—Spain—Ibieca—History—20th century.
2. Agriculture—Economic aspects—Spain—Ibieca—
History—20th century. I. Title.
HD1333.S712I243 1984   333.3'1'4655   83-21884
ISBN 0-8078-1594-2

Designed by Naomi P. Slifkin

for
Harold Friend Harding and
Elizabeth Reeves Harding

Contents

Contents

Illustrations

Maps

Tables

Preface

This is a study of how the men and women of Ibieca remade themselves, their families, and their village society between 1950 and 1975. More broadly, it is a study of social change in a capitalist dictatorship, of how market and state combined to transform one social order into another swiftly and surreptitiously. We shall see that the villagers of Ibieca unwittingly refashioned themselves and their world as they carried on what they experienced as life as usual. It is commonly assumed that industrial capitalist culture seduces preindustrial peoples to give up their ways of life in exchange for material goods and urban ambience. This study suggests instead that they participate willingly in social processes that dispossess them of their preindustrial cultures simply because they are unaware of what is at stake. Indeed, the villagers of Ibieca proceeded on the assumption that they were actually conserving their way of life.

The central transformative process, in Ibieca and in much of Spain, was an expansion of capitalist agriculture that was orchestrated by agrarian reform measures enacted under the regime of Francisco Franco. Villagers dismantled preindustrial forms of agriculture and constructed a form of mechanized capitalist agriculture through a series of separate, seemingly unconnected, individual decisions to alter their productive strategies in response to state subsidies and market-mediated incentives. The collective effect of these decisions was to dissolve the village and its homesteads as ecological, social, and moral universes, and thus to dispossess villagers of the experiential bases of their local culture and community. At the same time, villagers constructed a world in which agriculture was more a livelihood than a way of life, in which interdependencies within and between village families, and between families and the land, were eclipsed by more urban and market-oriented ties, and in which local domains of authority and solidarity gave way to more secular regional and national commitments.

For centuries the countrysides of the world have been trans-

formed by capitalist entrepreneurs as they altered rural market conditions, and by the direct intervention of state managers in the organization and conduct of agriculture. Ibieca's story sheds light on
how state and capital may collaborate and converge in remaking a
countryside, a powerful and frequent merger that is often obscured
for both participants and observers by laissez-faire preconceptions.
In effect, state managers under Franco assumed the role of capitalist
entrepreneurs as they enacted measures that mimicked and manipulated market conditions.

We also learn from the example of Ibieca the immense cooptive
power of such a merger. The social and cultural ramifications of
villagers' decisions to alter agricultural practices were unforeseen
and unintended by them, yet the decisions themselves were experienced as conscious and voluntary. Hence villagers inadvertently implicated themselves in dismantling their own way of life. The culturally corrosive power of the Invisible Hand lies in this discrepancy
between the individualized decisionmaking process engaged by the
market and the unforeseen collective consequences of that process:
people invariably get more than they bargained for. That power is
amplified under a dictatorship such as Franco's, in which people are
prohibited all access to political processes through which they
might foresee collective consequences and act collectively to resist
or reshape them.

Ibieca during the 1970s was a village in transition—not the village it once had been and not the one it was becoming, but a mixture of both, and hence a living record of its own remaking. During
my first summer in Ibieca, in 1970, I was struck by the stacking and
intersecting of disparate fragments of culture and history in the life
of the village. As I sketched a map of the village, I watched a crew of
workmen connect a network of pipes for running water and sewage
to run beneath village roads that had been trod upon by village
women, men, children, mules, horses, and sheep for at least eight
centuries. The orchards were littered with the wooden carcasses of
olive trees two and three centuries old, each toppled in a few min-
utes by giant tractors. One afternoon the young village priest,
Manuel Bueno, and I accompanied a half-dozen young villagers to
the thirteenth-century chapel in the fields not far from the village;
an hour later Manuel was exploring my impressions of Hegel,

Marcuse, and Hemingway, whose works he was reading. Daily I witnessed the expansion of contemporary capitalist culture and practice in the village, yet I discovered that villagers had participated in the most sweeping anarchist revolution in the world only thirty-five years before.

In the context of such juxtapositions of history and culture the focus of my fieldwork evolved into a reconstruction of recent village history and an excavation of the living past, through a combination of participant-observation of village life and in-depth interviews with most adult villagers. I lived in Ibieca for a total of twenty months between 1970 and 1973, and I have made four brief trips to the village since then. I arrived there by following a chain of scholars, priests, and schoolmasters from Ann Arbor to Madrid, Zaragoza, Huesca, and a half-dozen villages in the Somontano. For leading me to Ibieca and enabling me to stay there I thank Bill Christian, Carmelo Lisón-Tolosana, Moisés García-Sanz, Damian Iguacen Borau, María-Pilar Rubio, and Alfonso Malo.

Because this is a historical study I have not changed the name of the village, but I have changed the names of all the villagers. I have also interpreted their lives in ways they never intended. This account does not describe, but only reflects, the generosity, kindness, and patience that villagers bestowed on me during my stays in Ibieca. It is a most extraordinary gift to be permitted to witness people's lives. I am grateful to all the people of Ibieca, and most especially to those who sheltered me and gave me kinship: Concepción Martínez Bueno, Jacabo Salamero Betrán, María García Val, Santiago Salamero García, Concepción Esteban Alsina, and María Paz and José María Salamero Esteban. For shelter and kinship in Huesca I am equally grateful to Aurelio Biarge López, Josefina Lera Alsina, and María, Pedro, and Carlos Biarge Lera.

Scores of people in Spain and America have aided me in the conduct and completion of this project, and I am grateful to all of them. Harold, Elizabeth, Daniel, Joanne, and Robert Harding gave me courage and limitless berth. For their special contributions as scholars, critics, editors, and friends, I would like to thank Federico Balaguer, Charles Bright, Elizabeth Brumfiel, Davydd Greenwood, Carol Isen, Temma Kaplan, Edward Malefakis, Ellen Malcolm, Victor Mesalles, Rayna Rapp, Andrea Sankar, Michael Taussig, Charles

Tilly, and Marilyn Young. In Spain I owe special thanks to Aurelio Biarge, without whose vision this study would have been a shadow of itself, and, in America, to Bill Christian, Lynn Eden, and Roy Rappaport, without whose faith this book might never have been written.

Finally, I acknowledge and thank the agencies that have funded this study in its various stages: the Wenner-Gren Foundation, the University of Michigan Project for the Study of Social Networks in the Mediterranean, the Institute for Environmental Quality, the Rackham School of Graduate Studies at the University of Michigan, and the National Science Foundation.

Remaking Ibieca

✺ *Introduction*
✺ *The Worlds*
✺ *within the Village*

The children of Ibieca do not understand how their grandparents lived—what it was like to depend so intimately on the land, the weather, one's kin and neighbors; to walk to market in Huesca before day broke with a basket of eggs and a pair of rabbits; to respect death as if it were a living presence in the village. In Ibieca's history we may also glimpse our own, for many of our forebears lived in communities dismantled by the activities of capitalist entrepreneurs and statemaking politicians. Those communities and the processes by which they were dismantled varied in many of their details from Ibieca, but their histories have in common the destruction of ways of life unknown and unimaginable to those of us raised in the cities of the industrial world.

The recent history of Ibieca is the story of how one people fashioned and endured this transition. The major themes of my analysis are highlighted toward the end of this chapter. First, though, I shall introduce the village, villagers, and their story in more detail.

Place and People

Ibieca lies in the foothills of the Spanish Pyrenees, ten miles south of the Sierra de Guara. On clear days the welts on the rugged face of the dry southern slope are visible from the village. On other days the sierra becomes a somber, featureless form marking off the northern horizon with its peaks. Turning toward the south, the view from the village stretches far across an arid plain to the Monegros, an isolated, bleak range of low mountains. On a very clear day villagers can see a large monastery on a hilltop outside the town of Barbastro, twenty miles to the east of Ibieca; twelve miles to the west they can see Montearagón, a fort built during the Reconquest in the eleventh century on the outskirts of Huesca, the provincial capital.

The region between Barbastro and Huesca is known as the Somontano. It is a belt of foothills fifteen to twenty miles wide that stretches across the center of Huesca province, the northern province of the region of Aragon. A series of low mountain ranges, including the Sierra de Guara, compose the southern tier of the central Pyrenees and the northern border of the Somontano. To the south, the Somontano erodes into the plain that yields the Monegros mountains and becomes the Ebro River basin.

Although the terrain is rough and abrupt, broken into small ridges, mesas, ravines, and plains, the Somontano is liberally peppered with villages and about half the land is under cultivation. The Somontano's terrain and the temperate climate favor dry agriculture and a concentration of population in small villages. Over forty families lived in Ibieca when I was there in the early 1970s, all of them at least partially dependent on agriculture for their livelihood. The village itself is located at the center of its territory, and each day village men fan out to their family fields and orchards.

Relics of past centuries dot Ibieca's landscape. Most remarkable is an old church, transitional between Romanesque and Gothic in architecture, standing huge and silent in the fields a brief walk from the village. It was built around 1250 by Ximeno Foces, lord of Foces, a small village near the church that was deserted in the fifteenth century.[1] Ximeno Foces consecrated the church to Saint Michael in gratitude for his support in battles against the Moors in Valencia. A monument to their defeat, the church was built by Moorish prisoners of war and bears their stylistic influence. Like so much of Ibieca, St. Miguel de Foces is a hybrid of histories.

From a distance Ibieca appears to be an extension of the northern end of a mesa—a systematic rearrangement of natural colors, textures, and materials. Indeed, most of the building materials came from Ibieca's territory. Houses are built on foundations of giant stones cut from nearby quarries centuries ago, and the upper structures have been rebuilt several times since the stones were set in

---

1. The date of the church's construction is from del Arco, *Nuevas pinturas*, p. 6. I am grateful to Federico Balaguer, head of the Archivo Municipal de Huesca, for the date of the village's desertion.

Map 1. Northeastern Spain

place. Many of the bricks and roof tiles were produced by a small brick factory that quarried its raw materials on the village outskirts.

Most houses in the village are two stories tall. The first floor is a patio area that gives way to storage rooms and what used to be a stable, as well as to the street and the stairs. The kitchen, dining room, bathroom, and bedrooms are on the second floor. In some of the larger houses around the central plaza there is a full third floor

Ibieca with the Sierra de Guara in the background

with more bedrooms. The size of a house roughly indicates its family's position in the landholding hierarchy. Most village families own modest estates of less than 30 hectares and live in two-story houses. The three-story houses around the main plaza belong to wealthier families, and the only four-story house in Ibieca belongs to the Solano family, which owns nearly 300 hectares.

Village roads are fairly narrow and winding. They engender a sense that the village is bigger than it is, that it is complex and densely settled. Ibieca feels crowded but is not. In 1975 it had only half the population it had in 1900, when ninety families lived there. Older people can still recall who lived in which houses, many of them since converted to other uses. Entire categories of people and families have disappeared in recent decades: landless workers, beggars, charcoalmakers, blacksmiths, cartmakers, morticians, midwives, a herdsman for the common pasture, carpenters, and tailors.

Not many people die in Ibieca nowadays. They die in city hospitals, not in village houses, surrounded by doctors and nurses and machines, not by family and neighbors. When death does come to Ibieca, those present watch it closely; for them the experience of a villager's final moment becomes a symbol of his or her whole life.

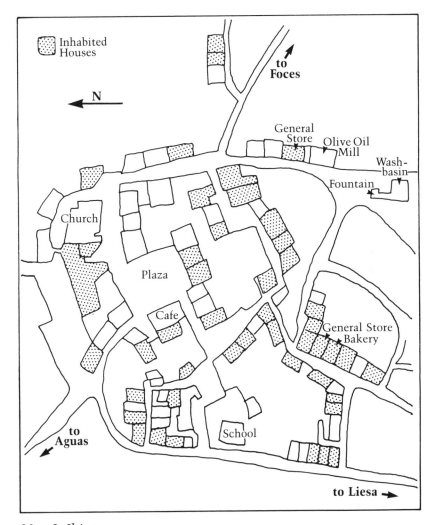

Map 2. Ibieca

Mourners describe a relative's death in vivid detail to all who offer condolences, and that description is often a marker, a trigger, for a life story in conversations that gather and mend the collective memory in years that follow. Villagers describe their history, their culture, and their society to each other as they recount the lives and deaths of kin and neighbors. They are not simply characterizing their social world; they are re-creating it.

In the warmth of Ibieca's late afternoon sun, elderly women often gathered around doorstoops, in semicircles of wicker and wooden chairs, to sew and to chat. The women who gathered around Angela's doorstoop were women with time on their hands. Angela and Julia were widowed; their children lived in Huesca, the provincial capital, and in Zaragoza. Catalina had never married and spent her adult life with her bachelor brother until he died; he was a tailor, she a seamstress. Engracia's husband was still alive but she was assisted at home by her widowed sister-in-law and her fifty-year-old bachelor son. Adora and her husband lived with their son and his wife, who took care of them. As the women sat around the doorstoop, their words sometimes meandered to a discussion of who was in the cemetery, when they had died, how, and what had become of their relatives. They mended their memories of village families with the thread of their talk, much as they were sewing up hems and cuffs and collars with the thread in their needles.

One of the women who used to sit around Angela's doorstoop, Julia, committed suicide in 1973. Villagers told her life through her death in the days that followed. Life storytelling in Ibieca creates continuity, solidarity, a sense of belonging; yet Julia's was the story of a woman who would not belong. The story of Julia's resistance to her social world can introduce us to that world, and to what it meant to be a woman in it.

Julia was seventy in 1973 and had lived alone since her husband's death five years before. One afternoon her neighbors realized she was missing. Angela, who lived a few houses away from her, triggered a search by asking others if they had seen Julia lately. Gradually it was determined that no one had seen her since late the previous afternoon, and within an hour it was concluded that she was missing. The specific events that occurred between the moment when her neighbors realized Julia was missing and the discovery of her body proceeded as if according to a script, although no one involved had ever experienced anything like it.

Since the door to Julia's house was locked and the key was on the inside ledge under the cathole, it was decided that she was probably not in the house. Since she left the key on the ledge rather than with a neighbor, it was decided that she had probably not left the village territory. The custom (hers and in general) was to leave the key with a neighbor along with word of where one was going and how long one would be gone. In Julia's case, if she would be gone more than a day, it was necessary as well as customary, because she had to ask someone to feed her chickens.

Those making the decisions at this point were near neighbors, both men and women. The discussion was concerned but not confused and far from panicked. Yes, the fact that she had not been seen was strange. Something might be wrong. It was time to enter the house. Perhaps she had passed out or was dead inside. Whatever was going on, it was for close relatives to discover, not neighbors. Her sons should enter the house first. The nearest neighbor with a phone called them in Huesca. Ramón was home at dinner. He said he had no idea where his mother was and that he would come right out. Later they reached Lorenzo, and one of Julia's neighbors drove to Huesca to get him.

By ten o'clock both sons were in Ibieca and they entered the house. She was not there. This dispelled the image of her hanging from an attic rafter, a rumor that was circulating around the village by this time. Still, where was she? More information soon emerged from the house. There were several odd notes scrawled on scraps of lesson-book paper and left on the kitchen table and counters. One, beside a few eggs and a loaf of bread, said, "Take these eggs and bread that Pilar gave me." Pilar was Ramón's wife. Others said: "Neither son is to blame for what I am doing." "Sons, I am sorry for the bad dinner I am going to give you." "Now there is nothing that anyone can do."

By this time her sons and a group of married men in their forties and fifties, neighbors and the village judge, were standing around the road outside Julia's house and making the decisions. The village territory should be searched, but first they would call the Civil Guards. It was clear that something had become of Julia, that she had probably tried to kill herself and was dead or dying somewhere in the vicinity. In the old days if there were any grounds for suspecting foul play in someone's death—and suicides were always suspected—relatives had to bribe local police and other authorities to avoid prosecution and get the body buried. That kind of thing was unlikely these days, but just the same it would be better if the police ordered and witnessed subsequent events because from then on they would be responsible.

The police arrived around midnight. They were told the facts, they read the notes, and then they ordered a search of the territory. Small groups of men with lanterns and flashlights went out, each toward a place where they thought she was likely to be found—ponds, basins, caves, and huts where she would not have been spotted during the day. Within a half-hour her body was found, and the church bells were rung to call the other groups back to the village. Julia's body was floating face up in a nine-foot basin that belonged to Casa Solano. One hand was clutching mud and grass from the bottom of the basin. A black scarf was tied around her head, covering her eyes. Her head was raised up out of the water by her clothes, which were puffed up around it. Her face was starkly white in contrast to the blackness of her clothes, the water, and the night.

It was decided to leave the body in the basin until the coroner could come. Groups of two or three men rotated watch by the basin until three o'clock, when the coroner called, officially waived his right to see the body as it was found, and told the police to have it taken up to the house. Julia's body was dragged out of the basin, wrapped in one of her own white bedsheets, brought up to her house on a pig-slaughtering rack, and laid on her bed. Everyone left the house, and the door was locked.

Villagers did not disguise their feelings about what had happened. Many expressed shame, knowing that all over the Somontano and in Huesca others were talking about the terrible deed and about Ibieca, where it had occurred. They also spoke freely about their fears, including men who said they had never before been frightened. Everyone was impresionado, "struck," by Julia's act of violence. Many did not feel Julia had the right to take her life and were morally repulsed. One woman told me that to seek death rather than to avoid it was unnatural for anyone but most unnatural for a woman.

Forces we did not know within us, or knew and wished to keep at bay, were released by Julia's suicide. I spent several sleepless nights lying in bed in a minor state of terror. Julia "visited" me on those nights, as she did many of the women and some of the men in the village. Each time I turned out the light I saw her form a few yards from my bed, standing just off the ground, dark and dripping wet, motionless, expressionless. She left when I turned the light on.

*Julia's sense of deliberateness, her careful planning and her un-
canny sense of exactly how and when her body would be discovered were most chilling. She had apparently killed herself during
the evening or night preceding the one of her discovery. The note to
her sons apologizing for giving them a bad dinner indicated that
she had calculated, correctly, that her neighbors would realize she
was missing by late the next afternoon and that they would call her
sons during dinner. Down at the basin she had taken off her shoes
and placed them on a nearby rock as if to say "I'm here" to search-
ers in the night. (Perhaps she did not realize that her body would be
floating on the surface by that time.) The notes in general conveyed
a ghastly calmness; their simple words begged for interpretation in
the context of her death. The one that said her sons were not to
blame for what she did neatly exonerated them from any legal cul-
pability while leading us to wonder about their moral and social
responsibility. Even her choice of where to kill herself was perhaps
not idle. The basin belonged to Casa Solano, the richest house in
the village, while Julia's was one of the poorest. During the Civil
War their families had been pitted against each other politically,
and they never resumed cordial relations.*

*Villagers expressed hostility toward Julia, in part because they
thought the violence she committed was aimed at them. Angela
and Julia's other close neighbors were angry at her and very critical
of her. One of the strongest social statements of their anger was
contained in the village women's refusal to dress Julia for burial.
Ordinarily neighbor women volunteer to dress a body for burial,
but this time no one came forth. When Ricardo Sánchez, the village judge, went to her neighbors' houses and asked women to
dress her, they refused.*

*Julia was buried in the sheet. Her act was seen as a denial of the
villagers' society, so they responded in kind, denying her their customs that make death a social experience. Many, in accord with
their feelings and with Catholic law, would also have denied her a
Catholic burial, but the village priest, Manuel Bueno, who was as
opposed to suicide on philosophic grounds as they were on social
grounds, gave her one in the name of charity. Villagers went to the
mass and joined her sons in carrying Julia's coffin to the cemetery,
but no one displayed the customary signs of grief.*

The village was in a kind of collective shock for several weeks after Julia's death. Her neighbors did not attempt an explicit explanation of Julia's suicide. Instead, they conducted a long collective conversation, in pairs and small groups, about Julia's life.

In 1926 Julia married Bernardo Loriente and moved into his house in nearby Bandaliés. He was the designated heir, so Bernardo and Julia were responsible for the care of his parents and his unmarried siblings who still lived at home. Julia did not like taking care of Bernardo's parents and siblings. She convinced her husband to renounce his inheritance, move with her to Huesca, and get a job. Julia's mother was visiting them from Ibieca when the Civil War started in 1936. As soon as it was clear that the war would be a long one, Julia and Bernardo decided to return to Ibieca with her and to live in her house with Julia's unmarried brother, Sebastián. Bernardo and Sebastián collaborated with the anarchists who occupied the Somontano for a year and a half during the war. Sebastián was a member of the revolutionary committee that governed Ibieca. Because of his collaboration, when the Nationalist army under General Francisco Franco took over the village, Sebastián fled to France in fear for his life and lived the rest of his years there in exile. Bernardo was not on the governing committee, but he and Julia were said to have abused, both verbally and materially, the general prerogative given them by their association with the anarchists. They reportedly called their neighbors fascists and profited from goods seized from them.

In the early 1950s Julia, who had two sons already, became pregnant again. She openly regretted it. In about the fourth or fifth month she secluded herself in her house for several weeks; when she emerged, she was no longer pregnant. The understanding was that she had given herself, or been given, an abortion. The two sons whom she did bear and raise ceased to speak to each other at some point, and it was said that Julia had turned them against each other. They spoke to one another as necessary on the days of her death and burial, then resumed their silence. When Julia's husband, Bernardo, had been sick and dying two years earlier, the doctor told her at one point that he would recover from the slight coma he was in. She complained, "I'm going to die before he does after all." Manuel Bueno, the priest, said, "From your words, one must think you want your husband to die now."

In the will that was written just before Bernardo's death, the house and lands, which Julia had inherited, were left to their younger son, Lorenzo. As long as Julia lived, however, she had the right to sell the patrimony if she came into financial need. Six weeks before her suicide, word went around the village that she had put the patrimony up for sale and that her older son, Ramón, had bought it. In other words, she put it up for sale as a way of switching heirs from Lorenzo to Ramón. Before the switch, she was on speaking terms with Lorenzo but not with Ramón. Afterward she spoke to Ramón, not to Lorenzo. At about the same time she also betrayed a friend in the village. She abruptly stopped speaking to a woman to whom she was distantly related and with whom she had been friends for years, instead turning her favor toward an unrelated woman who lived across the road from her.

For none of these deeds did villagers offer an explanation; they simply knew of them and reported them. Their reports did not draw conclusions, but in the context of their society and its rules the reports contained conclusions nonetheless: Julia was a bad daughter-in-law, a bad mother, a bad wife, and a bad friend. She broke the strongest rules of village life. Where the social structures gave her passage, she slammed the door.

Shortly before she died, Julia told me that her life was very sad and that she was *una figura*, a shadow of herself. She was a shadowy figure in two ways. First, Julia had not constructed a sense of herself in the terms given her by the village society of her youth and adulthood; second, by the time we talked, by the time she died, that social world was also a pale shadow of its former self. Julia and Bernardo had breached their obligations to his parents when they decided to move to Huesca, but a generation later, when Julia's sons married and moved to Huesca, leaving Julia and her husband alone, no moral judgments were passed on them. Julia and her sons lived in different social worlds, different moral universes. After his mother's death, Ramón sold the house to Catalans as a vacation home and built a big house with a swimming pool and a high brick wall around it on the outskirts of the village as his vacation home. No one said much about it. Ramón and his wife were not fettered by the expectations and obligations that circumscribed his mother. Julia's world was kept alive in the recollections of her peers, in their evocations of lives and deaths. It was no longer reproduced in social action, and it was not the prevailing social reality of Ibieca in the 1970s.

Two objects cannot occupy the same place at the same time, but two societies can, and do, in Ibieca. Village roads made of hard dirt were designed for draft animals and wooden carts, as well as for people. In 1970 they were serving motorcycles, cars, and tractors, and during the summer they were dug up by huge Caterpillar trenchers to lay pipes for running water and sewage. Some of the old stones above doors and windows have dates carved in them—1880, 1839, 1776—and many of the larger houses also have coats-of-arms representing titles which were probably purchased during the seventeenth and eighteenth centuries. Most houses were renovated during the 1970s: exteriors were plastered and painted, tiles replaced stones in the patio floors, veneered furniture for handmade, butane stoves instead of big, old-fashioned fireplaces, and a flush toilet for the old wooden board with a hole in it above the manure pile in the stable.

In the last thirty years a new society has been built into Ibieca's houses, roads, fields, social relations, roles, and identities. The old and the renovated houses embody distinct social relations of production. Family members and resident artisans produced most of the materials used in old houses from "free" raw materials available from their own land and village commons. In contrast, virtually all of the materials used in renovations were produced in far-flung factories by wage laborers and purchased in the city by villagers. The old houses embodied principles of self-sufficiency and production for use, whereas the renovated houses embody principles of market dependency and production for exchange.

As they rebuilt their houses, the men and women of Ibieca also remade their social world. They reorganized the conduct of agriculture, politics, family life, and religion. Julia's story gave us a glimpse of the vanishing world and one woman's experience in it. Stories from the lives of Mariano Castillo, Juan Solano, and their fathers show us the experiences of poor men and rich, in the old world and the new. Like Julia, Mariano and Juan's fathers were creatures of the old world, and their grandchildren are creatures of the new. Mariano and Juan themselves were among those who remade the social reality of Ibieca and thus represent the transformation.

Before the Spanish Civil War Daniel Castillo was a poor peasant, a sharecropper, and an agricultural wage laborer all at once. When he was not working for wages he worked the land he owned and sharecropped with a pair of mules, family labor, and an occasional hired hand. He harvested fruit and vegetables for his family's table, grapes for their wine, olives for their oil, and cereals for their bread and for his livestock's feed. In good years Daniel had small surpluses of wine, olive oil, and cereals to sell, but his first concern was to provide most of the food his family consumed. In the 1970s Daniel's son, Mariano, spent most of his time selling groceries, meats, and dry goods to his neighbors in his prosperous general store. Neither his family nor his neighbors produced much of the food they consumed, and Mariano reaped considerable profit from the shift. He still owned the land his father had passed on to him but he did not work it. Instead, Mariano hired his cousin to plow the land with a tractor and to harvest cereals with a combine. In the 1950s he uprooted most of the vines and olive trees, expanded his cereal fields, and planted several groves of almond trees. At that time cereals became a purely cash crop, as were almonds. With rising grain prices and increased crop areas and yields, Mariano increased the value of cereals produced on the Castillo estate fivefold between 1950 and 1975.

Mariano earned much more income from his store than from his land, but in his day his father, Daniel, had also depended on money from other sources for his family's well-being. Throughout the year Daniel sold his labor by the day to large landholders in the village. As had his father before him, Daniel often worked for Casa Solano for one or two pesetas, a loaf of bread, and a sardine each day. When Daniel's father needed money so badly one year that he decided to pawn a field, he turned to Luis Solano, who loaned him the money in exchange for use of the field. There was no way the Castillo family could repay the debt from income earned in Ibieca, so, rather than forfeit the field, for five consecutive years Daniel joined a team of reapers who earned peak wages working on the huge cereal estates in the south of the province.

In the years preceding the Civil War Daniel affiliated with the leftist faction in Ibieca, and when the war started he sided with the anarchists. They collectivized all the productive property in the village, and Daniel served as head of provisioning on the collec-

tive's governing committee. Mariano, who was in his early teens, ran the collective cooperative where food and goods were distributed. When Nationalist troops captured Ibieca, Daniel fled with Julia's husband and brother and a dozen other leftists, first to Barcelona, then to France. When he returned to Ibieca in 1940 he was sent to a concentration camp for six months. The next year Daniel and his two sons, Mariano and Jesús, set up a general store in the stable by their patio, adapting knowledge and skills acquired running the anarchist cooperative to capitalist commercial ends. The enterprise would be part of Mariano's inheritance. He traded on the postwar black market as well as on official markets to make it a financial success, buying and selling sheep, mules, wine, cereals, vegetables, and other foodstuffs in Ibieca, in surrounding villages and cities, and in the mountains to the north.

Mariano left his anarchist past still further behind when he married Sara Segarra, whose family was one of the wealthiest in the village and whose father had sided with the rightists during the Civil War. They were married in 1956 in one of the last old-fashioned weddings in the village. Their parents also made one of the last marriage contracts, documents which defined the economic underpinnings of a marriage in minute detail. Their contract stated how much money Sara brought to the marriage and that it would revert to her family if there were no children; it specified how much Mariano would pay his siblings when they married in return for their renouncing any further claims on the family estate; and it formally passed the Castillo estate on to Mariano, defining the rights of Daniel and his wife to its fruits as long as they lived.

Mariano was the oldest son and heir in his family and Sara was the oldest daughter of her family who stayed in Ibieca. Together they became the emotional center for both families over the years as their siblings married and moved out of their natal houses. On three of four holidays each year, Sara and Mariano invited their siblings' families to their home to feast on a huge midday meal. As their children grew up and went off to school, first to Huesca, then to Zaragoza, Lerida, and Barcelona for post-baccalaureate degrees, a gulf developed between them and their parents that dwarfed the one between Mariano's generation and his parents'.

On a holiday in July, 1979, I joined about two dozen family

Mariano Castillo and Sara Segarra on their wedding day, 1956

The Castillo family outside their house, 1971

members in Casa Castillo for the midday meal. The dinner was
long and elaborate, and both wine and food were plentiful. The two
generations of cousins, siblings, and in-laws sat at different tables,
one group of us in our teens, twenties, and thirties, and the other
group the parental generation. At our youthful table, as the excite-
ment of each other's company and the flow of wine loosened our
tongues, we launched an extended discussion of the issues of the
day—marriage, abortion, divorce, extramarital sex, and so on—
with everyone, except myself, outdoing each other with their liberal attitudes. Antonio said he and his girlfriend lived together and
had no intentions of marrying because in Spain, without divorce,
marriage was a form of bondage. José said he never planned to
marry and wanted to live in a commune. Everyone agreed that
abortion should be available to all women and that girls and boys
should have equal freedom to do as they liked. While we talked,

Sara Segarra and her sisters and sisters-in-law caught snatches of the conversation as they carried dishes to the kitchen, and their husbands caught every word as they sat with cigar smoke wafting around their heads.

When José Lacasa announced that no one should have to work if he did not want to, his father, Tomás, could resist no more. He joined our table and delivered a discourse of some breadth and substance on many of the issues his offspring and their cousins had so boldly broached. He argued that everything José enjoyed came from the relentless hard work of others, and that José's ideas about work were egotistical and destructive, as were most of the other ideas expressed at our table. Tomás was speaking out of and in defense of a way of life that was disappearing rapidly, though his children and their cousins could not recognize it behind his fury that afternoon. They thought Tomás was simply jealous of their options. Tomás, for his part, could not recognize that they were engaged in a collective process of evolving strategies to adapt to the new world that Tomás himself, Mariano, and their peers had ushered into Ibieca.

Villagers referred to Luis Solano as "amo Solano," which conveyed at once his economic, political, and social standing in the village. "Amo" meant owner, master, head of household, and boss; the term was applied to large landowners whose land was worked by wage laborers and sharecroppers, and who generally dominated village politics and government. In this latter capacity amos *were known as* caciques, *political bosses. Both* amos *and their wives refrained from manual labor—they were above it and above those who engaged in it—yet they were intimately tied to dozens of laboring families. Before the Civil War Casa Solano, with 300 hectares of land and four pairs of mules, hired five agricultural workers on yearly contracts, three day laborers on a regular basis, a score of workers during harvest seasons, and two shepherds, two domestic servants, and two errand boys on a full-time basis. The wage-labor relation in those days was fettered with other rights and obligations, among them an expectation that an* amo's *workers would support his faction in village politics. Luis Solano was the largest employer in Ibieca, supplying about one-third of its wage work, and*

Casa Solano

he used that role effectively to dominate elections and municipal government.

When anarchist and socialist militiamen entered Ibieca in 1936, shortly after the Civil War began, Luis Solano fled to Zaragoza, leaving behind his wife, Pilar Nueno, and six children. His family was in grave danger, but they survived. Twice neighbors watched through the cracks in their closed shutters as Pilar and her children were seized and loaded into a wagon while militiamen debated whether to kill them. One day they watched, some with horror, others with delight, as a militiaman paraded around the village streets in Pilar's wedding gown. The militiamen and their village allies were committed to an egalitarian society based on collectivization, and in launching it in Ibieca they took from the rich and gave to the poor. They confiscated all of Solano's productive property, assigned the Solano boys to work in the fields, and stripped the house bare, converting it into a storehouse and a home for war refugees and leaving Pilar and her children with only a small room. As the war went on, some villagers continued to harass Solano's family, but others discreetly favored them. Pilar and her children

*were shortchanged by some of those dispensing food and goods;
others made up for it by slipping her extra supplies.*

*When the Nationalists captured Ibieca in 1938, they called for
denunciations, testimonies against villagers who collaborated
with the anarchists. No one, not even Pilar Nueno, denounced anyone. Luis Solano returned the day after the village was taken. He
kept the collective's food and goods that had been stored in his
house for himself, and he reaped the harvests that had been sown
and tended with collective labor on his lands during the previous
months. He was appointed mayor and repealed the prewar distribution of common land to poor families, reaping those harvests for
himself as well. Usurping the redistributed common land was not
legal, but no one protested it or Luis's other abuses, lest he denounce them for their activities during the war. Pilar's information
about who had done what during the war was much more useful to
Luis as a way to control his enemies than as a means by which to
eliminate them. The animosity between Solano's family and some
of their neighbors was fierce enough so that Pilar and Luis stopped
speaking to them, and for years after the war Luis hired most of his
workers and servants from other villages. Although the spell of the
Solanos' authority in Ibieca was destroyed by the war, Luis recovered much of his structural power, economically and politically,
and it was passed on, with the family estate, to his son, Juan, when
he married in the early 1960s.*

*Like Mariano Castillo, Juan Solano transformed his father's es-
tate. In 1975 Casa Solano owned three tractors and one combine;
employed were two full-time tractor drivers, three day laborers,
two shepherds, and one domestic servant. Juan and his two adolescent sons worked every day alongside their workers, and his wife
worked alongside her servant. They were no longer "above" other
villagers, who referred to Juan and his wife by their first names.
The old interdependencies between the Solano family and other
village families based on exchanges of wages and labor, favors and
votes, had diminished markedly. Juan, who began managing the
estate with his father in the 1950s, invested early and heavily in
agricultural innovations, but his neighbors did not consider him
especially successful because most of his enterprises were barely
profitable, and some not at all. Juan Solano was somehow caught*

between old and new agrarian personas, modernizing enough to survive but not enough to prosper. Mariano Castillo estimated that Solano earned only half the income his estate was capable of producing.

As Solano's economic position and power eroded during the 1960s and 1970s, so did his political command of Ibieca. Mayors were appointed by the provincial governor after the Civil War until 1979, but the nature of the office and village politics were altered by governmental reforms, especially after 1962, while Juan was mayor. Essentially, the village political arena and its prerogatives shrank, and when Juan resisted the last phase of the process in 1973 he was replaced by Tomás Lacasa, who was younger and not beholden to Solano. After his dismissal Solano continued to hold enough sway to block some innovations his neighbors proposed and to continue reaping benefits of dubious legality. When mayorial elections were reestablished in 1979, he even regained the mayor's office after three candidates who garnered more votes than Solano did turned it down because they did not want to fight his influence or do his bidding. However, the political world of Ibieca, as of Spain generally, had changed radically between 1973 and 1979. Francisco Franco's dictatorship was replaced by a democracy, and most governmental offices and procedures underwent reform. It was a new regime, one in which Solano appeared more incompetent than corrupt, and which pressured him to represent the villagers' interests in ways that were foreign to him but that he struggled to learn.

Themes

While Julia Janovas resisted her social world, her sons and their peers, among them Mariano Castillo and Juan Solano, dismantled it and built a new one. Juan and Mariano converted the world of their parents, a world of peasants, *amos*, and workers, into a world of mechanized capitalist farmers.

The primary purpose of this study is to reconstruct the events and the processes by which this agrarian transformation occurred. How did the villagers of Ibieca remake agriculture between 1950 and

1975? The basic unit of agrarian production and social reproduction in Ibieca in 1950, and still in 1975, was the *casa*.[2] *Casa*, roughly translatable as "homestead," refers to the combination of people and property associated with a household—a family and its patrimony. The family includes members past and future as well as present, and the patrimony includes the house itself, furniture, stables, work animals, livestock, machinery, tools, fields, orchards, vineland, and financial wealth. It was toward the maintenance and reputation of the *casa* that village men and women, whether as peasants, *amos*, laborers, or farmers, bent their efforts—so much so that personal identities were submerged in *casas*, and personal needs were defined by the needs of the *casa*. Though much less so in 1975 than in 1950, the reputations and personalities of *casas* were the dominant social reality, and Ibieca was at least as much a community of *casas* as of individuals, or even of families.

My reconstruction of the agrarian transformation of Ibieca is primarily based on *casa* histories. I collected these from family members of all the village *casas*, and I conducted more intense interviews with a dozen village men regarding their agricultural practices. As I interpret these histories, villagers dismantled peasant and preindustrial forms of agricultural production and constructed a form of mechanized capitalist production through a series of discrete, individual decisions during the 1950s and 1960s. They were attempting to alter their productive strategies in response to state subsidies and market incentives, and the ramifications of many of these decisions were unforeseen and unintended by villagers, whose common goal was the survival and prosperity of their *casas*. In a sense, they "backed into" advanced capitalist agriculture and the social world that came with it. Experientially, the *casa* was the eye of the storm of agrarian change, but, as we shall see, it was remade as much as was the social and political life of the village.

This study has a number of secondary purposes, some of which I

2. The *casa* is the basic cell of village society all over upper Aragon; see Pujadas and Comas, "La 'Casa.'" It seems to have been in the French Pyrenees as well. In Emmanuel LeRoy Ladurie's words, in fourteenth-century Montaillou "the family of flesh and blood and the house of wood, stone and daub were one and the same thing. . . . The essential concept of *domus*, the domestic group of co-residents involved various subordinate elements: the kitchen, fire, goods and lands, children and conjugal alliances" (*Montaillou*, pp. 24–25).

pursue explicitly, some of which are more submerged in the structure of the text and in the historical narrative. Briefly, they are as follows.

My analysis of agriculture in Ibieca implies a critique of analyses which describe the recent transformation of Spanish agriculture as moving from "traditional" to "modern," or from "precapitalist" or "peasant" to "capitalist" agriculture.[3] While I think there was a rupture between the agricultural practice of 1950 and 1975, the labels "traditional" versus "modern" serve only to characterize and evaluate the practices, not to analyze them. Nor does the distinction between "precapitalist," or "peasant," versus "capitalist" agriculture work. Agriculture in Ibieca in 1950 (indeed, in 1850) was not precapitalist; rather, it combined the preindustrial labor-intensive, capitalist agricultural practice of *amos* with much less market-oriented peasant agricultural practice. By 1975 both forms of agriculture had been displaced by the mechanized, or capital-intensive, capitalist agricultural practice of farmers.

Much of the American literature on village Spain appeals to "modernization theory" to explain the manifold changes that have occurred in the countryside during the last few decades.[4] One way or another, the reasoning goes, Spanish villagers were exposed to urban goods, comforts, and values; they changed their behavior, including their agricultural practices, in order to gratify newly acquired urban tastes. The "rural exodus" is usually stressed as a major causal force, since it increased the urban connections of villagers, and so is urban industrialization, since it drew emigrants from villages.

My reconstruction of Ibieca's history argues that the order of change was reversed. Villagers changed their productive behavior

3. These labels are usually relied on as a shorthand, not as categories of conscientious economic and historical analysis. Most Spanish village studies focus on social and cultural practices and treat agriculture as part of the background. Also, villages vary as to their mix of agricultural practices—some are in fact composed entirely of small landholding peasants. Davydd Greenwood, in *Unrewarding Wealth*, and Juan Martínez-Alier, in *Labourers and Landowners*, have done careful economic and historical studies of agriculture, Greenwood of small landholders in a Basque town, and Martínez-Alier of large landholders and laborers in Cordoba.

4. See, for example, Aceves, *Social Change*, and Barrett, *Benabarre*.

long before they encountered capitalist consumer culture, for which many adults never acquired a taste, and change was well underway before the "rural exodus" of the 1960s. My study supports the critics of "modernization theory" who argue for the centrality of changing market conditions in such historical transformations, and it amends their position, in Ibieca's case, by arguing just as forcefully for the centrality of state policies and programs. State agencies under Francisco Franco did not intervene directly in Ibieca to induce or coerce change in agrarian practice, but they manipulated market conditions and other incentives so thoroughly that the state was the arbiter of Ibieca's recent history. With the exception of studies by Edward Hansen and Eduardo Sevilla-Guzmán,[5] the state's role in shaping recent rural history in Spain is generally underestimated.

My interpretive realignments are the outcome of my historical reconstruction of social change in Ibieca and the Somontano. If anthropologists expect to contribute anything of lasting value to the theoretical and descriptive literature on social change, we will have to become historians as well. We cannot infer the past from the structures of the present which our anthropological training equips us to analyze. With relatively minor adjustments in field techniques, plus a study of documentary and secondary sources, we *can* capture the structured process that is the history of the people among whom we live.

I have included many stories from the lives of villagers in this account, partly to breathe life into it, partly out of a respect for the integrity of villagers' experience, and partly to make two more points about the study of social change: people, not structures, make both society and history. History is structured—people do not make it exactly as they please—and in making history people also remake social structures. We cannot understand social structures as they are lived—what people actually do and do not do, and therefore how social structures are re-created, transformed, and abandoned—unless we somehow include the diversity of individual personalities, actual social relationships, and historical experiences in our studies.

5. Hansen, *Rural Catalonia*; Guzmán, *Evolución del camesianado.*

Some of the stories I gathered from villagers and from living in the village became little mysteries to me, stories which I needed to interpret in order to understand the experiential significance of the recent agrarian transformation. What was the significance of the dismissal of Juan Solano as mayor in 1973, and of his election in 1979? Why was there such an intense conflict over morals between the two generations of siblings and cousins dining in Casa Castillo? What were the social and cultural structures otherwise fading from daily village life so powerfully evoked by Julia's suicide? The solutions to these and other small mysteries lead me to conclude that agrarian reform was part of, and in some respects the cause of, a broader transformation of life in Ibieca, one that included the demise of the *caciquismo* and the dissolution of social ties and ethics which bound village and *casa* as moral universes. That a way of life is passing in the Spanish countryside is not a new assertion, and I do not mean to romanticize or regret in any way the end of the poverty and the oppression associated with that way of life. John Berger argues that the historic role of capitalism is "to destroy history, to sever every link with the past and to orient all effort and imagination to that which is about to occur."[6] My study of Ibieca is at once an investigation of that process in one community and, insofar as I succeed in reconstructing the past and the passing way of life, a protest against it.

Finally, I conclude from this study that agrarian reforms are never merely the programs for economic well-being but are always political programs as well, programs for restructuring rural class relations and the relationship between a state and its rural peoples. This aspect of an agrarian reform effort is exceptionally well disguised when most of the measures are translated into market or marketlike mechanisms, as were the measures which remade Somontano agriculture. The Invisible Hand of the market masked the social consequences of tiny, seemingly unconnected individual decisions to alter one's conduct of agriculture, and later of domestic life, in response to market incentives. The gradual and irrevocable repatterning of social life within and between *casas* between 1950 and

6. Berger, *Pig Earth*, p. 213.

1975 was an epiphenomenon of actions taken to preserve and improve a way of life, not to change it beyond recognition. The stealth of the market, combined with the irresistibility of state reforms under Franco's dictatorship, made for an awesomely quick and quiet cultural dispossession in the Spanish countryside.

Agriculture in Ibieca before 1950 was not static, and Chapters 1 and 2 of this study reconstruct the recent history of preindustrial capitalist and peasant agriculture in the village and in the Somontano. Chapter 1 makes the point that we need not appeal to unique forces to explain the contemporary transformation of Ibieca. Villagers did not have to change their mentalities in order to adapt their productive strategies to new conditions under Franco; rather, they had been adjusting their productive strategies to changing conditions for centuries. Chapter 2 scrutinizes the two-year period during the Spanish Civil War when the villagers of Ibieca radically reorganized their agriculture according to anarchist design. It is a story in its own right, one deprived of much significance in village history by Franco's victory, but it reminds us that that subsequent history was not inevitable. The contemporary history of Ibieca, and of Spain, could have been (and almost was) very different, if not by anarchist design, then by socialist, or communist, or Republican design.

Chapter 3 pauses in the Ibieca of 1950, reconstructing social life within and between *casas* before the agrarian reform. Chapters 4 and 5 update Chapter 1. Chapter 4 describes how the historical context of village agriculture was transformed between 1950 and 1975, largely by state agrarian reforms. Chapter 5 details the reorganization of village agriculture, its conversion from preindustrial capitalist and peasant forms to a mechanized capitalist form, and the central role of the *casa* in that transformation. Chapter 6 is in dialogue with Chapter 3, showing how the social organization of the *casa* and village were ultimately remade during the agrarian reform process.

Chapter 7 describes and interprets the debates among village men about the prospect of forming an agrarian cooperative in Ibieca. The usual formulas for explaining villagers' reluctance to form a cooperative, such as "amoral familism" and "peasant individualism," pale in the context of Ibieca's history and social organization, and we are left finally with a sense of the open-endedness of the village's future. In the Conclusion I argue that the social and political consequences were not incidental side effects of the agrarian reforms, but the fact that they were experienced as such was one of the special powers of the wedding of state and market under Franco.

Part One
Peasant, Lord,
Laborer, and Amo:
The Somontano
before 1950

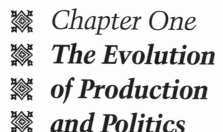

Chapter One
The Evolution
of Production
and Politics

In Aragon during the nineteenth and early twentieth centuries there were two main forms of agricultural production. In the peasant form of agriculture, owner and worker were one and the same, and the primary goal of production was to supply household needs. In the early, or preindustrial, capitalist form of production, landowners (amos) hired wage laborers to produce crops primarily for market sale. Amos also produced to consume, and peasants also produced for sale, but as secondary activities. What distinguished early from later capitalist production was that it was labor intensive, not capital intensive, and that the wage-labor relation was embedded in elaborate social rights and obligations and was not conceived of as a mere exchange of wages for labor.

These general features characterized peasant and early capitalist forms of production all over Spain. However, the forms varied considerably in each region depending on its political, economic, and cultural history, on the other forms of agriculture and manufacturing in the region, and on the region's relationship to national and international economic structures. In the high mountain areas of upper and lower Aragon peasant forms organized most agricultural activity, while in the broad plains of the Ebro basin early capitalist organization predominated. In foothills zones such as the Somontano a balance was struck between the two forms—they were mixed, interdependent, and roughly equal in their impact on the organization of ways of life.

The peasant and early capitalist productive forms dominated the Somontano countryside for more than a century after feudal claims and forms of production were abolished all over Spain in the early 1800s. During subsequent decades the early capitalist form first expanded, then contracted, then rallied somewhat in the 1920s and again in the 1940s. The peasant form seems to have held steady and then expanded around the turn of the century when the early capitalist form was waning. There were some other changes over the period—increases and decreases in village populations and particular social categories, the introduction of some small hand-operated machines, improved plows, and a new cash crop, almonds. Overall, however, the two prevailing productive forms retained their basic shape and relationship to each other until 1950. If there was a shift, it was a slight one that tipped the balance of power and authority away from large landowners, but by no means transferred it to small landowners.

In this chapter we shall survey the feudal origins of peasant and *amo*/laborer productive forms, review the course of their development, and assess how the policies and organization of the Spanish state affected that course during the nineteenth and early twentieth centuries. This historical review shows that the period prior to the Franco reforms was hardly static. The people of rural Aragon generally, and the villagers of Ibieca in particular, were continually adapting their strategies of agricultural production to changing conditions of market and state. Villagers had participated in the dismantling of feudal productive relations only a century before. The ensuing balance of peasant and early capitalist productive forms which structured political and social relations within Somontano villages until the Civil War depended on broader political and economic conditions that sustained and limited each form, conditions such as weak markets for crops and credit, ample and cheap labor, and a political system that linked rural political power to control over labor. As those conditions shifted, especially after 1900, so did the balance, not enough to recast the system of productive relations in the Aragonese countryside, but enough to move the principal rural elites, large landowners, steadily into a more defensive position.

Feudal Dominion

The agricultural focus in the Somontano on olives, grapes, and cereals, and probably the village settlement pattern, date from

Roman occupation of the area. The only major crops introduced since Roman times were the potato, in the eighteenth century, and almond trees, in the early twentieth.

The association of the peasantry with another form of production also dates back at least to the Roman occupation, when peasants were connected to a system of villas that employed local labor. During the early Middle Ages they were connected to Visigothic, then Muslim, overlords. No written records reveal the extent and nature of the connections between peasantry and overlords in the Somontano until the twelfth century, when the area came under seignorial domain that lasted until the early nineteenth century. The peasantry was fairly free during the whole feudal period: peasants held title to their land, passed it on to their heirs, and, with their lord's permission, could buy and sell land. Not all lords, who were clerics, nobles, and military men, owned land in villages under their domain, but all gathered their dues in crops, money, and labor, appointed village officers, and administered justice.

The first documentary evidence from Ibieca is a will which passed seignorial domain over the village from Galin Garcés de Arturella to his son, Xemeno.[1] The will is dated 1154, about a half-century after the area was reconquered from the Muslims. During the sixteenth century Ibieca, and Liesa to the south, were under the domain of Juan Gurrea. Most villages surrounding Ibieca were under the domain of other secular lords or clerical institutions. In the Somontano more generally in the sixteenth century, about half of the villages were under the domain of secular lords, a quarter under clerical lords, and a quarter under royal domain.[2] Most of the territory of Casbas was owned by clerical institutions, while the lord of Ibieca owned a large house on the plaza and a few fields.[3]

In 1656 Don José de Moncayo took "true, present and physical possession" of Liesa in a ritual display of his power that was re-

---

1. I am grateful to Federico Balaguer, head of the Archivo Municipal de Huesca, for knowledge of this will.

2. Durán Guidol, *Geografía medieval*, pp. 19–22.

3. I am grateful to Aurelio Biarge, a provincial historian, for this information, which he determined from announcements in the Official Bulletin of Huesca Province during the 1840s and 1850s, when feudal landholdings were auctioned by the state.

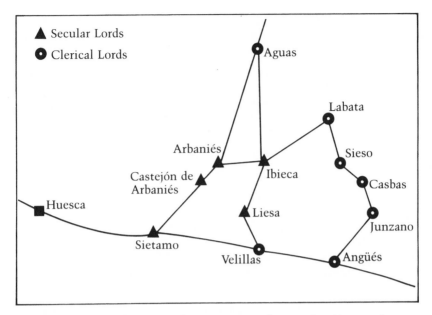

Map 3. Lords in the Central Somontano during the Sixteenth Century

Source: Duran Guidol, *Geografía medieval*, pp. 56ff.

peated in his other seignories, including Ibieca.[4] The lord "took possession" as he walked through the village streets, opening and entering granaries, and through the fields, uprooting plants. He demonstrated his judicial power as he ordered a wooden gallows built in the central plaza and performed a symbolic execution, then gathered the village councillors before him on their knees and asked them to swear their loyalty and to fulfill all their obligations to him.

A century later, when Don José de Moncayo's descendant, the Conde de Fuentes, took possession of his seignories, the ceremonies had changed. When the lord took possession of Almuniente, about thirty kilometers south of Ibieca, in 1745, he toured the village and entered the granaries, but he did not uproot plants. He dismissed and reappointed the mayor, but he did not order the symbolic execu-

4. The description of this ritual and the next one are from Aznar Navarro, "Los señores aragoneses," pp. 930–40. See also Domínguez Ortiz, *Sociedad española*, pp. 315ff.

tion. Rather than extracting an oath of allegiance from kneeling village councillors, the Conde de Fuentes listened as Almuniente's Sindico Procurador, a royal appointed representative of the count's vassals, stood before him and publicly protested various seignorial rights such as the monopoly on grain storage and grape pressing, the hemp tax, and the annual payment of thirty-three hens.

The difference between the ceremonies of 1656 and 1745 represents the growth of the Spanish state on the local level in Aragon. The turning point came in 1707, when the kingdom of Aragon was defeated during the War of Succession, and the victorious Bourbon king, Philip V, abolished the local law codes of Aragon for its support of his Hapsburg rival. In 1716 the king abolished the criminal and some of the civil jurisdiction of Aragonese lords and gave their vassals full recourse to royal courts. During the eighteenth century the crown checked seignorial control of municipal governments, first by establishing qualifications for the offices of mayor and judge, later by creating new offices, such as that of Sindico, to give voice to vassals in municipal government, especially on matters of food supply, use of public lands, grain storage, and conscription.[5]

The union of Aragon and Castile dates from the marriage of Ferdinand of Aragon and Isabella of Castile in 1469. However, the kingdoms were largely autonomous until the eighteenth century, when Castile incorporated Aragon institutionally by measures such as those described above. One of the principal results was the growth of a nonfeudal elite in the Aragonese countryside, one that challenged seignorial dominance using the political mechanisms provided by the crown. The power of the rising elite, composed of large landowners, merchants, and millers, was amplified by eighteenth-century economic and demographic trends.

Mostly due to a declining death rate, the Spanish population increased during the eighteenth century by over 40 percent, from 7.5 million inhabitants in 1717 to 10.5 million in 1797. Ibieca's population more than doubled between 1717 and 1838, from 150 to 324 inhabitants.[6] Prices fluctuated for the first half of the century, then rose more or less steadily, increasing 35 percent between 1750 and

5. Domínguez Ortiz, *Sociedad española*, pp. 309, 322, 341, and 358.
6. Nadal, *Población española*, p. 16, on Spanish population. See Appendix, Table 1, on Ibieca's population.

1790.[7] The increasing demand for food reflected in the rising prices pressured landowners to put more land into cultivation, and much common land was put to plow spontaneously, bypassing both law and custom.

During the eighteenth century there was considerable struggle in many areas over which social groups would benefit from the expansion of agriculture.[8] Seignorial political and judicial rights and obligations were gradually absorbed by the crown and its representatives, but lords maintained most of their economic rights. In the early nineteenth century the descendants of the Conde de Fuentes were still collecting one-ninth of all crops, fees for use of the village olive mill and oven, and several days' labor per household from their Somontano domains.[9]

Aside from seignorial domain, the major feudal rights still intact in Spain were entailment and mortmain. In 1800 36 percent of Spanish territory was entailed, or held inalienably by family lines which passed their estates on from generation to generation through single heirs. Another 32 percent of the territory was bound by mortmain—held in perpetuity by monasteries, convents, parish churches, and educational institutions.[10] In other words, fully 68 percent of Spanish land was protected from market forces by feudal privilege. The proportion was lower in the Somontano, probably less than 50 percent, but it was no less a landed basis for the dominance of feudal lords in the countryside.[11]

These pillars of feudalism in Spain—entailment, mortmain, and seignorial domain—survived eighteenth-century reform efforts. Then, between 1808 and 1854, constitutional governments dismantled the juridicial and political apparatus of feudalism and tore out its landed basis. State decrees abolished the privileges of entailment, mortmain, and seignorial domain. All the lands of the church, military orders, and charities, and some of the royal and municipal lands, were expropriated and sold at provincial auctions

7. Herr, *Eighteenth-Century Revolution*, p. 87.

8. Herr, *Spain*, pp. 58–59; Casas Torres, *Aragón*, pp. 51ff.

9. Madoz, *Diccionario geográfico*, 6:86.

10. Based on figures in Carr, *Spain*, p. 39, and Simón Segura, *Desamortización*, p. 220.

11. Based on figures in Simón Segura, *Desamortización*, pp. 158–59, 220, 246.

to private owners. Privately held marketable land increased from 32 percent to 87 percent of the total, and the complex web of rights and obligations between lord and peasant was wiped away.[12] Although who benefited most from the land sales varied across Spain, the combined effect of the sales and political reforms was to transfer dominant control of land, labor, and rural government to private landowners, merchants, and millers—the nonfeudal elite cultivated during the eighteenth century.

In some Somontano villages land transfers from feudal lords to (for the most part) wealthy landowners were substantial. In Ibieca, however, the passing of seven centuries of feudal dominion involved no substantial land transfer because the Conde de Fuentes owned only a few fields in the village. Rather, reform involved the abolition of feudal dues, administration, and justice; and, according to several elderly villagers who recalled stories their grandparents had told them, the count's house in the plaza was sacked and burned to the ground. The event marked the unfettering of both *amo*/laborer and peasant agriculture of their feudal obligations.

Early Capitalist and Peasant Agriculture

During the nineteenth century Spain's population grew from 10.5 to 18.6 million,[13] and with it grew the demand for agricultural products. In only a few areas, such as the Cordoba River valley, was that demand translated into an intensification of agriculture through private investments. For the most part, it was translated into an expansion of land under cultivation. According to Vicens Vives, between 1818 and 1860 land under cultivation in Spain increased by 4 million hectares, or about 25 percent.[14] The trend reversed around 1860; between 1860 and 1900 cultivated land de-

12. The newly marketable land was broken down as follows: 36 percent of the national territory was disentailed, as was 12 percent held by clerical institutions, and 7 percent held by civil corporations was auctioned. See Carr, *Spain*, p. 39, and Simón Segura, *Desamortización*, p. 220.

13. Nadal, *Población española*, p. 16.

14. Vicens Vives, *Manual de historia*, p. 578.

creased by 3 million hectares. Most of the new land put into cultivation before 1860 and later taken out was devoted to cereals. Land devoted to vines and olive trees, on the other hand, continued to expand after 1860, increasing by about 1 million hectares between 1860 and 1900.[15] The expansion of vineyards was stimulated by French demand from 1880 to 1900, after French vineyards were destroyed by phylloxera and before new disease-resistant stocks were producing, and it was reversed as phylloxera spread through Spain at the end of the century.

In Huesca most of this agricultural expansion was carried out by large landowners, in response to growing markets and the general unfettering of landownership and land use resulting from anti-feudal reforms. The growth in the size of the landless labor force indicates that early capitalist productive relations expanded during the first part of the nineteenth century. In 1787 landless laborers constituted about 40 percent of the agricultural workforce of the province, and in 1877 they were 59 percent.[16]

The subsequent phase, from the late nineteenth century to World War I, was one of crisis and contraction of capitalist agriculture. Newspaper articles and editorials for the 1890s in Huesca bemoaned hard times in the countryside, citing bad weather, low prices, emigration, and soil exhaustion as the causes.[17] The growth of industries, such as textiles in and around Barcelona, pulled immigrants from Huesca province, while the collapse of French demand for wine in the 1890s, and the vine blight's spread through the Somontano a decade later, pushed emigrants out.

The populations of Ibieca and the Somontano declined from the end of the nineteenth century on, with land-poor and landless families making up the majority of emigrants. In 1860 39 out of Ibieca's 90 houses were landless, while in 1940 20 out of 75 were landless. The birth rate was dropping faster than the death rate, which also contributed to the decline of Somontano village populations. The

---

15. Ibid., p. 581.

16. The 1787 figure is for the whole region of Aragon (Ministerio de Estado, *Censo de 1787*), and the 1877 figure is for Huesca province only (Instituto Geográphico y Estadístico, *Censo de 1877*). In 1877 the proportion of workers in the agricultural labor force for all of Aragon was 61 percent.

17. *Diario de Huesca*, 1892 and 1895.

average number of children born to Ibieca families who survived infancy fell from 3.5 to 2 between 1890 and 1950.[18]

Landownership in Ibieca

The Somontano is not considered a latifundia district because its large estates are relatively small, and it is not considered a minifundia district because its small estates are relatively large. The Somontano landholding pattern is a mixture of moderate versions of both land tenure patterns. Most of the land is held in large estates (30-100 hectares) and in true latifundia (over 100 hectares) which, until 1950, were worked largely by wage laborers. The majority of landowners, however, had small estates (3-10 hectares) and true minifundia (under 3 hectares), which they worked with household labor largely for household consumption. Owners of medium estates (10-30 hectares) hired wage laborers when family labor was insufficient. Ibieca's landholding pattern illustrates both the mix of early capitalist and peasant productive forms and the rough balance struck between them in the Somontano. (See Table 1.)

While the growth of Ibieca's population during the mid-nineteenth century indicates the expansion of *amo*/laborer relations of production, we may infer a subsequent contraction of those relations and an expansion of the peasant form of production from cadastral information. Most landless families depended on agricultural wage work on large estates, and between 1860 and 1960 twenty-seven landless families left Ibieca or bought land. Among the landholding categories, the sharpest decline between 1860 and 1960 was in the number of minifundia owners, who were virtually as dependent on agricultural wages as were landless villagers, whereas the number of small estate owners increased substantially, from five to twenty-three.

Information on the size of landholdings confirms the expansion of peasant production and indicates another important shift, a concentration of land by large estate owners at the expense of medium estate owners. (See Table 2.) Both the amount of land held by medium estate owners and the average size of medium estates de-

18. Calculated from Ibieca family histories, from the number of surviving siblings per generation.

Table 1. Land Distribution in Ibieca, 1860 and 1960

| | Number of Holders | | | |
Landholding Category	1860	%	1960	%
Landless Houses	39	44	12	17
Minifundia (under 3 hectares)	18	20	10	15
Small Estate (3–10 hectares)	5	6	23	33
Medium Estate (10–30 hectares)	18	20	13	19
Large Estate (30–100 hectares)	8	9	10	15
Latifundia (over 100 hectares)	1	1	1	1
Total Landed Houses	50	56	57	83
Total Landed and Landless Houses	89	100	69	100

Source: Based on the 1860 cadaster and 1960 land records kept by the village government.

creased markedly over the hundred-year period, as did the number of medium estate owners, from 18 to 13. (See Table 1.) These trends and those indicating expansion of large and small estates suggest a polarization in the forms of production. Small owners operating primarily as peasants and large owners operating primarily as early capitalists had the best chances of surviving between 1860 and 1960.

Some of the new peasant owners were upward-mobile landless laborers and minifundia owners. They continued to work part-time for large landowners. Combining all three categories, the proportion of village households with labor available for hire by large landowners only declined from 70 percent in 1860 to 65 percent in 1960. The difference, of course, was that in 1860 most of those households were completely dependent on wage work for their subsistence, whereas in 1960 most of them had sufficient land to survive without regular wage work. Sales of municipal land and lotteries of common lands between 1860 and 1960 increased the amount of privately held land by over 100 hectares; the lotteries probably facilitated some of the upward mobility of minifundia owners, and

Table 2. Hectares in Landholding Categories in Ibieca, 1860 and 1960

Landholding Category	1860		1960	
	Total	Average Size	Total	Average Size
Minifundia	26	1.4	18	1.8
Small Estate	32	6.4	142	6.2
Medium Estate	383	21	193	15
Large Estate	340	42	489	49
Latifundia	218		282	

Source: Based on the 1860 cadaster and 1960 village land records.

land sales probably produced some of the increase in large land-holdings. The rest of the expansion of land owned by small and large estate owners came from the contraction of land held by medium owners (383 to 193 hectares). Stories were still told in the 1970s of the decline of these houses—of Casa Abadías, Casa Panzano, Casa Capablo, and Casa Bierge. Their owners had been compelled to sell off their lands to other houses at below market prices in order to pay debts and dowries.

Contemporary villagers could not recount stories of the decline of medium landholding houses in much detail, because families scatter and memories fade when houses close. Casa Bandrés and Casa Castro were two modestly wealthy houses that survived the rocky economic shoals of the turn of the twentieth century through propitious marriage and the relentless labor of Andrés Castro. We can also see, in the story of Castro's wife's great-grandfather, how Casa Bandrés was built up during the early nineteenth century.

Andrés Castro and Sebastiana Bandrés were born in Ibieca around 1900. They lived in Sebastiana's house, much of which was closed off, and the rest was sparsely furnished and decorated. It was a cold winter day in 1972 when we talked, sitting by the fireplace in broken-down wooden chairs. Andrés did all the talking about their family histories, with Sebastiana occasionally joining in to offer us a piece of ham and some crackers, or perhaps a glass of wine.

Carlos Bandrés, Sebastiana's great-grandfather, was born in Ibieca around 1800. He and his wife married without any inheritance on either side (casado solteros) and built up a patrimony of twenty hectares from trading food and goods. Carlos became a muleteer, gathering surplus wine from houses in the Somontano in his cart and transporting it across the sierras, to Aragüés del Puerta, Paternuy, and other high mountain villages. Word traveled of his arrival in a village and men came in from surrounding hamlets to buy his wine, paying in cash. He left unsold wine at a local tavern for the innkeeper to sell in his name, and he bought potatoes, beans, soap, salt cod, and rabbits to sell back in the Somontano. Carlos made these arduous trips, each one four or five days long, continuously in spring and fall as long as the mountain passes were snow free. In July and early August he took his mule team up to sierra villages to thresh wheat for a fee after he had threshed his own.

Carlos and his wife had four children. His only son and heir, Domingo, continued muleteering and working family lands through the end of the nineteenth century, and he and his wife had four children. Domingo's oldest son and heir, Juan, gave up muleteering at the turn of the century and devoted himself to working family lands after his father was killed in a fall while working in the fields. Juan married a few years later and his wife had two children, both daughters. In 1929 Juan helped arrange the marriage of his eldest daughter, Josefina, to Andrés Castro—a propitious marriage, because Andrés was also heir to a substantial estate, and Andrés and Juan expected they would be better off working their estates together than separately.

Andrés was heir to a forty-hectare estate. His father was one of eight children, seven of them daughters. One daughter became a nun and the other six married into landholding houses in the Somontano, all of them drawing dowries from Casa Castro's wealth. The only son, Manuel, was heir to Casa Castro. He married three times. His first wife died without bearing children. When Manuel was in his fifties he remarried and his second wife bore three children. Andrés and his twin brother were born in 1903, when Manuel was sixty; their mother died a month later of a heart attack when she heard Andrés screaming in the kitchen and thought he had fallen into the fireplace. (When Andrés told me this, he said he was responsible for his mother's death.) A few years later Manuel married for a third time, but he died shortly thereafter, when the twins were five. The house and children were left in the hands of his third wife, Rafaela, who was not a hard worker and "put on airs." She drank cognac and wine, spent money on luxuries, and let the land go to weeds for eight years.

Only the mercy of the tax collector saved their estate. The tax collector could have confiscated the property in lieu of unpaid taxes but did not, Andrés recalls, simply because he was kind and let them go each year after a cup of wine at their house. Andrés's twin brother left home at eleven to find work in Huesca and rarely returned after that. At twelve Andrés decided he would revive the family estate. First he bought a team of oxen, which cost around 3,000 pesetas in 1915. He sold 40 sheep and 200 olive trees of Casa Solano for half what they were worth (he did not know the value of property, or how to negotiate) in order to raise the money. Andrés sharecropped part of the estate, and with his team of oxen he proceeded to work the remaining fields and orchards day and night until his house was finally out of debt seven years later.

His estate was in good shape when he married Josefina Bandrés, but their marriage was not a long one. Josefina died in childbirth, and the child died two years later. The deaths broke the link between the Bandrés and Castro families; however, they were rejoined shortly, in 1932, when Andrés married Juan's younger daughter, Sebastiana.

In the stories of Casa Bandrés and Casa Castro we can see how much the fate of village families depended on the timing and circumstances of birth, marriage, and death, and on the habits of hard work and frugality of family members. The fate of families, especially those with substantial holdings, was also tied to fluctuating markets for their crops and livestock. As we shall see in the following section, for example, phylloxera struck Ibieca's vineyards and the foreign market for cheap Spanish wine collapsed just as Manuel

Castro's first and second wives died and not long after the *casa* had been drained by dowries for his six sisters.

Crops and Livestock

Even though the amount of privately held land increased in Ibieca between 1860 and 1960, the amount of land under cultivation decreased. In 1860 village households cultivated over 800 hectares, while in 1945 they cultivated 700 hectares.[19] Not all crop areas decreased. Paralleling the overall pattern in Spain, vineyards and cereal lands decreased and almond and olive groves expanded.

During the late nineteenth century the whole Somontano experienced a wine boom; in 1900 eleven representatives from Angüés, the district's commercial center, attended a wine exposition in Paris.[20] In 1860 there were 204 hectares in vineyards in Ibieca, and the area no doubt expanded during subsequent decades. Before phylloxera struck, at least nine houses in Ibieca produced 6,500 to 10,000 liters of wine in an average year. The blight ended the boom, and although resistant stocks were soon available, the credit necessary to recover and get back on a commercial track apparently was not. The recovery of French vineyards soon precluded any reexpansion of commercial wine production in Spain, except in areas of elite viniculture.[21] The 61 hectares listed in vines in the 1945 cadaster was still more than enough to supply village demand. In 1954 another blight struck village vineyards; it was not as deadly, but it left the village capable of meeting only half of its own demand.[22]

Cadastral information and villagers indicate an overall contraction in land devoted to cereals after 1860. It is difficult to determine

19. See Appendix, Table 2, on crop areas.

20. *Diario de Huesca*, no. 7114, January 30, 1900.

21. According to Aurelio Biarge, the provincial *caciques* who dominated the wheat market and owned giant wheat-growing estates also controlled what little credit was available from Huesca capital, and they refused to loan it to vinegrowers on reasonable terms.

22. From a report to the Ministerio de Hacienda de Huesca from Ibieca's council asking to be relieved of paying taxes in 1956 because of, among other things, losses suffered from the 1954 vine blight.

the extent of the contraction; however, it probably did not affect the village's capacity to meet its demand for bread and feed. The land taken out of cultivation was the poorest yielding, and the subsistence needs of the village shrank with the declining population. In spite of the contraction of cereal lands, it is likely that, because of higher market prices, cereals were more important as a cash crop for many village households in the 1940s and 1950s than they had been in 1860.

The 1860 cadaster registered 31 hectares in olive groves, while 82 hectares were listed in olive groves in 1945, plus 17 hectares in almond groves. Almond trees were introduced in the village in the 1920s, shortly after a monk in a Barbastro monastery grafted a new variety capable of resisting local frosts. Most of the expansion of both olives and almonds probably occurred during the 1920s, carried out mainly by large and medium landholding houses aiming to produce more surplus for market sale. One large landholding house, Casa Sánchez, reportedly "struck it rich" with almond groves in the 1920s.

Meat consumption in Ibieca before the 1950s was very low, especially for poor families, and within families not all members ate meat equally. Angela Iglesias, whose family was both poor and large, proudly described giving up an egg or a piece of meat over and over again so that her husband or children could have more. Most village houses raised a pig for slaughter, curing and making sweetbreads and sausages. Slaughtered in December or January, the pigs supplied meat through the following year, above all during the cereal harvest in July and August, when men in particular were working hardest.

Small livestock raised in household stables provided another source of meat. All houses raised some chickens and kept a few hens for eggs. Some wealthier houses had large flocks of chickens, and many houses kept rabbits, pigeons, and ducks. Hunting was a supplementary source of meat: rabbits, hares, quails, partridges, and an occasional boar ran wild in the village countryside.

Around 1900 Casa Solano bought some cows and began selling milk to villagers who could afford it. In the late 1920s and early 1930s there was a minor milk boom as six more houses, all of them belonging to medium or large landholders, bought a cow or two. Only Casa Segarra and Casa Solano survived the 1930s and continued to supply the village with milk.

In 1950, as in 1860, there were two flocks of sheep and goats in Ibieca. The village collective flock decreased from 700 to about 275, while Casa Solano's flock was about the same size, some 250 head. Every summer shepherds took the flocks up to the high mountains for pasturing in villages which, in turn, sent their flocks down to the Somontano in the winter. Solano and the village collective made separate arrangements with mountain villages, one of a number of such exchanges. Mountain villages raised most of the work animals that foothill villagers bought to plow their fields, and regular trips in fall and spring by foothill muleteers, such as Carlos and Domingo Bandrés, supplied mountain and sierra villages with wheat, wine, and olive oil.

The Organization of Agricultural Work

A hundred years ago all households in Ibieca used a set of techniques and tools to cultivate and harvest cereals that had probably not changed much in centuries. In early winter men pushed a big iron plow, drawn by a pair of oxen or mules, across their fields, then walked up and down the rows broadcasting cereal seed, and finally turned the soil over the rows again with their work animals and plow. In spring they returned with their work animals to harrow the fields and to clear them of weeds. In late June, just as the heat was becoming unbearable, the men cut the ripened stalks with a sickle, while others, including women and older children, followed behind them making bundles. The bundles were tied into sheaves and transported in a cart to the threshing ground. Most landholding houses had their own threshing ground and threshing occupied long days for whole families from mid-July through August. The grain was separated from the stalks by cutting them up with a threshing sled (*trillo*) that had iron blades and sharp stones driven into the bottom and was drawn by draft animals with the driver standing on top of it to give it weight. The threshed cereal was gathered and then laboriously winnowed by tossing it into the wind with wooden pitchforks. The wind caught the chaff, blowing it away, and the grain fell to the ground. A final cleaning of the grain was done with large sieves, to remove the last of the chaff.

The old system of agriculture was enormously labor intensive. Few landed houses were so matched to their family labor supply that they neither bought nor sold labor. The medium and large land-holding *casas* hired laborers at some time during the year, and a number of them had year-round hired hands, *mozos*, as well. The small estate and minifundia holders and landless houses provided laborers, either by the year or by the day. The fluctuating needs of families hiring and selling labor yielded a very mobile workforce. The story of Eugenio Clavero illustrates that mobility among agricultural laborers and the hardship of their lives.

Eugenio and I sat at the kitchen table while his daughter, Antonia, prepared vegetables for the evening meal. Later, when her husband and son came in from the fields, she served us ham, bread, and wine. Eugenio was eighty-five. His legs had buckled from sixty-five years of hard labor in the Somontano and he could hardly walk, but his memory was clear and quick.

Eugenio was born in 1887 in Abiego, a village east of Ibieca. When Eugenio was ten he went to work as an errand boy (chulo) for a wealthy family in Bierge, and he continued to work for wages until he was seventy-five. By the time he was twenty-five Eugenio had worked his way up from errand boy to ox driver (buyatero), to mule driver (mozo de mulas), to foreman (mozo mayor). As was the custom in the Somontano each Saint Michael's Day, September 29th, he either verbally renegotiated his contract with his amo or he moved on, looking for a job in another house. Eugenio first came to Ibieca in 1905, at seventeen, and worked as an ox driver for a year in Casa Castro, shortly after Andrés and his twin brother were born. It was a memorable year—there was a measles epidemic and twenty-two children in Ibieca died. Eugenio worked in other villages for the next decade and returned to Ibieca in 1915, this time to sharecrop part of the Castro patrimony with a first cousin.

That year Eugenio met Aurora Haya, and he married her in 1917. Aurora, an only child, inherited a small house and a few hectares from her parents. Not long after their wedding Eugenio's widowed father married Aurora's widowed mother and came to live in Casa Haya. Aurora bore three children, dying of pneumonia a few months after her youngest child died. Five years later Aurora's mother burned to death when she caught fire at the kitchen hearth, leaving her daughter, Antonia, at thirteen, to care for her brother, father, and grandfather. Eugenio's family was to suffer still one more tragic death—his only son, who had helped organize and run the anarchist collective in Ibieca during the Civil War, fled before Nationalist troops captured the village and was killed in the Battle of the Ebro.

During his life Eugenio worked in more than a dozen houses as an agricultural laborer, usually for two or three years at a time. In addition, he had at least a half-dozen nonagricultural jobs—as a ranger in Esquedas, in a French bomb factory near the border during World War I, as a handyman for a power plant in a Catalan mountain town, and in a small brick and tile factory in Ibieca. After he married Eugenio took year-round jobs in Ibieca houses. In the 1920s he worked in Casa Blanco, during the 1930s in Casa Segarra, and during the 1940s in Casa Solano. From 1919 to 1936 he and his father and several other men from Ibieca walked to Vicién, south of Huesca capital, and reaped cereals for large estate owners for peak seasonal wages of ten pesetas a day.

Aside from family and wage labor, sharecropping was a common arrangement for working land.[23] Villagers estimate that 10 to 20 percent of the land was once sharecropped. Small and medium estate owners who had emigrated or were short on household labor sharecropped their entire estates, and large landowners sharecropped individual fields, vineyards, and orchards. Most sharecroppers were themselves usually small landholders. The sharecropper put in his family's labor, a team of draft animals and, in the case of cereals, half the seed. The landowner paid the land taxes and half the cost of seed. Customarily owner and sharecropper split cereal harvests evenly; the owners got three-fourths of the crop from vines and trees.

23. Villagers use the same term to describe sharecropping and renting: *arrendar.* They often refer to sharecropping as *arrendar a medias.*

The school children of Ibieca, around 1930

Early in this century a number of mechanical innovations in the harvesting of cereals were adopted by landed houses in the village. Although they had been introduced in the province at the end of the nineteenth century, it was 1920 before steel disc threshing sleds and scythes fully replaced the old sleds and sickles in Ibieca. During the 1920s many landed houses acquired mechanized reaping machines (*segadoras*) that were drawn by draft animals, as well as hand-powered winnowing machines (*aventadoras*). In 1926 Luis Solano bought a huge dragon-like motorized thresher (*trilladora*) that both threshed and winnowed cereals, spewing grain out of its spout. In 1947 Tomás Coronas, a medium landholder, bought another.

Several of the early technical innovations in cereal harvesting significantly reduced the demand for labor. Although the disc threshing sleds and scythes probably did not drastically reduce the number of man-hours per hectare, the reaping and winnowing machines, which were adopted by about a dozen landowners, cut their labor demand in cereal production by about a tenth—perhaps twenty hours per hectare. The two landowners who combined their threshing and winnowing in the threshing machines cut their demand by more than 25 percent. (See Table 3.)

The period of these earlier innovations in cereal harvesting was also one of absolute decline in the size of the labor force in Ibieca and in the number of work animals. I have already indicated that most of the houses that closed during the hundred-year period were heavily dependent on wage work for their livelihood. Table 4 shows the decline in terms of the male labor force and the number of work animals in Ibieca. The total population, the size of the male labor force, and the number of work animals declined by 35 to 40 percent between 1860 and 1955.

We can see the overall effect of these trends on agricultural production in Ibieca and on the balance between the two forms of production. Although the size of the male labor force did not decline much faster than the labor saved by new machinery before the Civil War, the male labor force was less available for wage labor as poor and landless houses increased their landholdings. In addition, large landholding houses expanded their production of almonds and olives, both highly labor intensive crops unaffected by early mechanical innovations. Less labor was available, yet more labor-intensive

Table 3. Labor Required by Early Methods of Cereal Production

Methods	Preharvest Man-hours	Harvest Man-hours	Total Man-hours
Sickle, Threshing Sled, Pitchfork	74	108	182
Reaping and Winnowing Machines	74	88	162
Reaping and Threshing Machines	74	63	137

Source: Man-hours per technique from my observations in Torres de Calatayud in Zaragoza province, where labor-intensive methods were still in use in 1972; from conversations with villagers in Ibieca; and from Ministerio de Agricultura, *Coeficientes horarios*.

Table 4. Ibieca's Population, Work Animals, and Male Labor, 1860 and 1955

Year	Total Population	Males 15–65 Years Old	Work Animals
1860	398	137	138
1955	262	89	84

Source: Based on the 1860 cadaster and on 1857 and 1955 census data.

crops were being cultivated. The combined effect was a contraction of the area under cultivation in Ibieca between 1860 and 1955. Land cultivated by peasant families expanded with their fourfold increase in numbers, so the land taken out of cultivation belonged to medium and large landowners. Capitalist landowners adapted to changing conditions by mechanizing and shifting to more lucrative cash crops, but they nevertheless lost some economic ground in relation to the peasant form of production.

Agricultural Credit and the Cereals Market

Before the Civil war began in 1936, only Casa Solano had bought a mechanical thresher. Why did other large landowners allow their land to go out of cultivation rather than mechanize production? The uncertainty of the wheat market and the absence of credit for capital improvement were two considerations precluding or at least discouraging full mechanization. The cereals market was controlled by middlemen, flour millers, and the owners of huge estates—veritable wheat barons—on the plain south and west of the provincial capital. Together they formed a major faction in the provincial power structure, and the cereals market, which mainly traded wheat, was one of their power bases. As in the rest of Spain, "most of the cereal was produced by small holders who were victimized by unfair terms imposed on them by middlemen and flour millers speculating on a fall in prices."[24]

Latifundia owners in the Somontano were in a better position to bargain for a good price because they had more to sell and because they were often themselves involved in wheat marketing or closely connected to someone who was. Other villagers, small and large holders alike, apparently had no trouble selling their wheat, but the market was risky and unpredictable. It did not inspire the kind of confidence required to devote a larger portion of arable land to commercial cereal production, or to invest in innovations that would increase productivity.

The principal reasons why villagers borrowed money before the war were crop failure, loss of work animals, and, in the case of more substantial holders, daughters' dowries. Given the kind of credit available, to resort to it was sometimes a disaster in itself. If a wheat crop was bad one year, small landholding houses that had no surplus to sell used their next year's seed for bread flour and had to borrow enough seed from larger landholders in order to sow and reap and eat again. The standard seed-borrowing arrangement in prewar Ibieca was *la dobla*—for every tray of seed borrowed, two were due the following year. With an interest rate of as much as 100 percent,

---

24. Tamames, *Estructura económica*, p. 90.

the borrower was likely to be in a similar position the following year, unless the weather was good. If the weather was so bad for several years that the borrower kept falling deeper in dept, he or she would eventually have to forfeit a field.

When a landholder needed cash, the common arrangement was *la carta de gracia*. The landholder put up a field as collateral on a loan which was due in a set number of years. During that period the creditor—another landholder in the village or a neighboring one—used the field, and its usufruct served as the interest on the loan. If the loan could not be repaid when it was due, the field was forfeited to the creditor. Finally, ordinary loans were available at high interest rates from usurers who lived in the village, or, on a smaller scale and at somewhat more reasonable terms, from *amos* for their workers.

In sum, money was scarce and expensive in the village before the Civil War. There was little available for investment, and even large holders often had to borrow just to meet their traditional obligations. Angela Iglesias said her family was so poor that they could not call a doctor when someone was dying, but they called a veterinarian if their mule was sick. They could manage without the person, but not without the mule.

Various reform programs undertaken by Spanish governments in the late nineteenth and early twentieth centuries attempted and failed to ameliorate these market and credit conditions, as well as broader political and social conditions, in the countryside. Sometimes because of, and sometimes despite, the reform efforts, large landowners lost ground politically as well as economically during the period.

State Reforms and Caciquismo before the Civil War

Until the 1930s, the intervention of the Spanish government in the organization of rural society was, for the most part, limited to the manipulation of land use rights, livestock privileges, inheritance rights, taxes, tariffs, price and wage controls, and to small-scale irrigation and land reform schemes.[25] Spanish governments also affected agricultural activity indirectly through the maintenance and reorganization of juridical and political institutions in the countryside.

The nineteenth-century constitutional governments that dismantled feudal institutions turned over dominant control of land, labor, and rural governments to a class of private large landowners, substantial merchants, and educated elites. Private power domains in the countryside were not encapsulated by the organization of the state through the process. Instead, state political resources and institutions were absorbed by the evolving preindustrial agrarian capitalist elite, the *caciques*. Overall, early nineteenth century state reforms institutionalized *caciquismo*, the political dominance of preindustrial capitalists in the countryside. The early capitalist form of production expanded in the sense of extending production to new land before 1860, but not in the sense of intensifying production. Nor did productivity increase after 1860, despite various state efforts to alter internal economic and political conditions.

The problem was especially acute in the case of cereal production, which engaged over three-quarters of Spanish agriculturists. After 1860 agriculturalists in the United States, Canada, and northern Europe were producing wheat at such low costs that, even with transportation costs added, they could undersell Spanish wheat growers in the coastal markets of Spain. The Spanish state responded with a wheat tariff which enabled domestic producers to survive but acted as a disincentive for them to change their methods of production. With the emergence of a trans-Atlantic world wheat market in the 1870s and 1880s, areas that could not compete with the world wheat price shifted to other economic activities or increased subsistence production.[26] The Somontano and Spain in

25. My general sources for this section and the next are: Herr, *Spain*; Vicens Vives, *Manual de historia*; Kaplan, *Anarchists of Andalusia*; Simón Segura, *Desamortización*; Malefakis, *Agrarian Reform*; Tamames, *Estructura económica*; Tamames, *República*; López de Sebastián, *Política agraria*; Fernández Clemente, *Aragon contemporaneo*; Aya, *Missed Revolution*; Kern, "Spanish Caciquismo"; and Kern, *Liberals, Reformers, and Caciques*.

26. Friedman, "World Market," p. 7.

general were not competitive, and market wheat production waned while subsistence production waxed. These world economic processes underlay the fourfold increase in peasant households and the contraction of early capitalist agricultural production in Ibieca between 1860 and the Civil War.

State juridical and political reforms amplified the political power of early capitalist producers in the countryside during the nineteenth century, while developments in the capitalist world economy resulted in an expansion of peasant relations of production around the turn of the century. Although *amos* maintained their grip on rural political structures into the twentieth century, their public posture and exercise of power became more defensive.

Aside from tariffs, state policies and programs aimed directly at agriculture during the nineteenth century were limited and ineffective. The efforts failed not only because they were inadequate and ill designed, but also because they were corrupted by the politics of early capitalist production itself. In 1877, for example, the Spanish parliament passed a law to subsidize a reorganization of the country's grain cooperatives, which were in a financial crisis due to the decline in cereal production. In Vicens Vives's words, the law was "twisted by the facts of political life into a financial base for *caciquismo*."[27] By the end of the century it was fairly clear that the general expansion of capitalist agriculture was over and that *caciquismo* was a major force blocking further development based on capital investments.

The control of *amos* over labor opportunities in villages and towns, and hence over votes, was the basis of their power in the larger political system. As *caciques*—political bosses and patrons—they provided access to government resources and benefits to their client-laborers in exchange for their votes for representatives in the national parliament.[28] During the Restoration, between 1876 and

27. Vicens Vives, *Manual de historia*, p. 579.

28. Some studies of social hierarchy and power relations in Spanish villages use the concepts of patron and client; see Pitt-Rivers, *People of the Sierra*; Kenny, "Patterns of Patronage," "Power Structures," and *Spanish Tapestry*; Aceves, *Social Change*; and Barrett, "Social Hierarchy." Other studies do not; see Lisón-Tolosana, *Belmonte*, and Martínez-Alier, *Labourers and Landowners*. The difference seems to be that the former emphasize political relations, and the latter, economic relations. It may be

1923, Spain was governed by a constitutional monarchy that relied on *caciquismo* to organize electoral politics in the countryside. The governing political parties, Liberal and Conservative, were allied with two somewhat fluid factions of local elites on the provincial and municipal levels. Party leaders in Madrid decided which party would win control of the government, and the necessary votes were organized on the local level by allied *caciques*. In return, they had special access to the apparatus of government while their party was in power, including control over provincial and municipal governments. The fact that their political power rested on control over a dependent labor force gave latifundia owners a vested interest in stalling the development of capital-intensive agriculture in the countryside. And their control over municipal government and electoral politics gave them the means of foiling state efforts to develop capitalist agriculture. Finally, the dependence of national politicians on caciqual politics for their own political survival crippled reform efforts at the top.

During the early twentieth century the efforts of Spanish governments to reform agrarian productive and political structures went through three phases. The first decade of the century saw efforts at political reform which would break caciqual power in the countryside. The aim was to restructure municipal government in such a way as to diminish the hold of *caciques* and increase the participation of medium and small holders, who would animate agrarian society and revitalize the Spanish political system. This administrative reform effort rarely got beyond impassioned debates in the Spanish parliament and completely failed to effect any changes on the local level.

The next effort was conducted by Primo de Rivera's government. The only widespread agricultural boom during the early twentieth century was stimulated by foreign demand during World War I and collapsed as soon as the war was over. Primo de Rivera, an army

---

that the differing analyses reflect differing realities. In Ibieca, political power was so clearly derived from and secondary to economic power that I have avoided the concepts of patron and client, which emphasize the political aspect of the relations between social groups. Also, *amo* (not *patrón*) is the term used in the village to refer to powerful men.

general, declared himself dictator a few years after the economic slump began, managed a recovery, and was removed from office in 1929, just as the capitalist world system plunged into the Great Depression. To consolidate his power, Primo de Rivera suspended the formal caciqual apparatus by dissolving the parliament and dismissing provincial civil governors and local government officers. The mayors appointed by his government came from outside the *cacique* cliques; they operated in terms of an official government party, the Patriotic Union, which was "apolitical." While these moves neutralized the rural oligarchy, they did not attack it directly; nor did the strictly agrarian reforms pursued by Primo de Rivera's government, though they were substantial relative to previous state reforms. His government built a modern system of roads, installed electricity in the majority of villages, built dams which irrigated whole new tracts of land, and set up credit institutions to finance agricultural investments. Given more time, perhaps these policies would have developed capitalist agriculture. As it was, they and the agricultural development they stimulated were abruptly cut short by the Great Depression.

During the Second Republic, between 1931 and 1936, there were several attempts at rural reform. The major program focused on the expropriation of large estates. These were to be divided and sold to land-poor and landless workers, who would repay the government in long-term installments from profits they made selling produce. Republican reforms also targeted rent, wages, and hiring practices, again endeavoring to help land-poor and landless workers. These efforts mobilized opposition both from large landowners, whose estates were threatened, and from anarchist organizations, whose aim was the collectivization, not the redistribution, of expropriated estates. Conflicts over agrarian reforms produced many crises and probably the demise of the Second Republic. Even had there been more consensus on ways and means, however, the Republicans were hamstrung by lack of funds. The amount of land actually expropriated and sold to small landholders was relatively small and its effects imperceptible when the Second Republic was overthrown by Franco's coup in 1936.

The efflorescence of political and economic reform programs

aimed at breaking the grip of *caciquismo* on the Spanish country-side all failed or were curtailed by larger events. Still, the growth of rival political parties and unions changed the world in which *caciques* ruled. So did the successive reorganizations of the Spanish state, first robbing *caciques* of the electoral arena under Primo de Rivera's dictatorship, then filling it with empowered rivals under the Second Republic. In Ibieca the caciqual factions weathered the shifting structures but were barely holding their own against challenges from the Republican and radical left when the Civil War began.

The Liberal and Conservative parties of the nineteenth century did not represent different policies so much as different personnel, competing networks of support radiating from Madrid through provincial capitals and electoral districts to villages and towns. In Huesca province there were five electoral districts, each dominated by rival *caciques* who allied with village-level *caciques* during elections. Village *caciques* were not obliged to one party and could shift allegiance to the district or provincial boss who promised them most, although many did develop enduring loyalties. During the late nineteenth and early twentieth centuries the hegemony of the Liberal and Conservative parties was compromised as rival parties and factions formed on the provincial and national level, some supporting the monarchy, some a republic, and others a revolution.

In the early twentieth century Luis Solano and the heads of the next two largest landholding houses, Casa Blanco and Casa Costa, were the principal political bosses in Ibieca. The Liberal party dominated parliamentary elections in Huesca until 1910, and Solano and Blanco were its henchmen. In the elections of 1899, 1901, and 1905, all of Ibieca's more than 100 votes were recorded as going to Manuel Camo, the Liberal candidate. Before the 1910 election Clemente Costa launched a rival political faction committed to Miguel Moya, a monarchist with vague Republican sympathies, on the Independent Republican party ticket. There was no Liberal candidate that year, and Moya won the provincial election. He won two-thirds of the vote in Ibieca, the other third (most likely representing what was left of Solano and Blanco's following) going to a Carlist candidate. Moya, and later his son, won the 1914, 1920, and 1923 elections by similar margins against candidates from the ultra-conservative Agrarian party.[29]

The competition between the Costa and Solano-Blanco factions was stiff, and stories linger in Ibieca about vote-buying and tamperings with electoral results. According to one story, in the 1920 election Guillermo Lobera, who had voted for Solano's candidates in prior elections, switched to Costa's after Lobera married Costa's niece. Solano had been renting Lobera a piece of land for his brick factory, and after that election Solano threw Lobera off his property. Lobera's loss was more than compensated for by Costa, who promptly turned over another piece of land to him, rent free.

Relative to earlier elections, those under the Republic were free of caciqual dominance, but factional competition was no less fierce. Villagers formed branches of two Republican parties, the Radical Socialists and the Spanish Confederation of Independent Rightists (CEDA). In the 1931 parliamentary election left-liberal candidates (Radical Socialists) received two-thirds of Ibieca's votes, with the other one-third split between center (Radical) and right (Independent) candidates. In the 1933 and 1936 elections, in which women voted for the first time, the village's votes were divided evenly between left and right coalition candidates.

The political factions in Ibieca were rooted in the organization of village agricultural production, and the balance of power between them was structured both by various market conditions and by the organization of the state. Under the constitutional monarchy, *amo*/laborer relations of production endorsed caciqual factions and a hierarchical worldview in which the rich ruled the village politically by reason of their superior status. Peasant relations of production issued more egalitarian and democratic sentiments and a worldview in which either all or none ruled, but this perspective was submerged as long as the *caciques* held sway. The caciqual factions dominated Ibieca until the Second Republic, when electoral battles resulted in an uneasy standoff between parties on the right and left and their respective worldviews. As we shall see in the next chapter, during the Civil War the left briefly prevailed and radically reconstructed Ibieca to reflect egalitarian principles of social order.

29. I am grateful to Luis Germán, an Aragonese political economist, for electoral information from Ibieca and Huesca before the Civil War.

❀ Chapter Two
❀ Civil War and
❀ Anarchist Revolution
❀ in Ibieca

The Spanish Civil War was a welter of complex struggles.[1] In the world political arena it was the locus of an escalating international struggle involving the United States, Great Britain, France, the Soviet Union, Germany, and Italy over fascism and the fate of liberal democracies. Within Spain it was a struggle between two national coalitions of interests for control of the state. The forces loyal to the Republic included workers and much of the urban middle class, while the rebel Nationalists under General Francisco Franco were supported by most of the urban and rural upper classes, the clergy, and the military. In some areas peasants' loyalties were predominantly sympathetic to the Republic; in others they were pro-Franco. In many areas, such as Aragon, villages were more evenly divided in their loyalties.

On the local level, in some zones loyal to the Republic, the war became a laboratory for the most intense and widespread experiments in anarchist revolution ever conducted. Most thoroughly in the northeastern regions—Aragon, Catalonia, and Valencia—a revolution in economic, political, and social structures was conducted

1. My main sources on the Second Republic, Civil War, and social revolution, aside from field data, are: Bolloten, *Grand Camouflage*; Bookchin, *Spanish Anarchists*; Borkenau, *Spanish Cockpit*; Brenan, *Spanish Labyrinth*; Chomsky, *American Power and the New Mandarins*; Fraser, *In Hiding*, "Revolutionary Committees," and *Blood of Spain*; Jackson, *Spanish Republic* and "Living Experience"; Kaplan, *Anarchists of Andalusia*; Malefakis, *Agrarian Reform*, "Internal Political Problems," and "Peasants, Politics, and Civil War"; Mintz, *Anarchists of Casas Viejas*; Moore, *Social Origins of Dictatorship and Democracy*; Orwell, *Homage to Catalonia*; Peirats, *CNT*; Souchy, *Entre los campesinos*; Thomas, "Anarchist Agrarian Collectives." I also studied the collection of documents and newspapers from Aragonese towns and villages gathered by Nationalist troops as they conquered the area; these are stored in the Civil War archives in Salamanca.

in the midst of the war. Ibieca was one of hundreds of villages that participated. This chapter describes Ibieca's experience in detail and interprets it in light of some of the literature on anarchist revolts in other villages. I suggest that the loss of *casa* autonomy under the anarchist regime was grievous to many villagers, and that while the anarchist revolution succeeded organizationally, it was caught in a serious contradiction between its commitments to free will and to collectivization, at least in Aragon, where understandings of freedom and *casa* autonomy were so intertwined.

For Ibieca, as for the rest of Spain, the Civil War began when Franco revolted against the Second Republic on July 18, 1936. The resident Civil Guards in Angüés declared support for Franco and within a week had rounded up and shot forty local young men accused of leftist or Republican sympathies. The executions terrorized those who supported the Republic in Ibieca, while rumors that militia columns were forming in east-coast cities and preparing to reestablish Republican control in the countryside struck fear in the hearts of rightist sympathizers. During these early days most villagers hid their food and valuables and slept in the fields at night so that they could flee quickly if necessary. Luis Solano punctured his olive oil kegs, saying, "If I can't have it, no one can." Villagers were appalled by his wastefulness and afraid that, if militiamen saw the stain left by the oil, they would take reprisals. Several times villagers gathered spontaneously in the central plaza to exchange rumors and discuss the importance of not betraying each other regardless of what happened.

Ibieca's fate was determined by the outcome of skirmishes and battles elsewhere. When Franco declared his coup, the workers of Barcelona, Tarragona, Castellon, and Valencia organized resistance and within a few days secured their cities for the Republic. The militia columns they formed during the first week headed for the Aragonese capitals—Teruel, Zaragoza, and Huesca—which had all been taken for Franco by resident military and police forces. The columns were stopped on the outskirts of all three provincial capitals around mid-August, and the Aragonese front was thus established. It held until March, 1938, when Franco's Nationalist troops broke through and captured eastern Aragon. Ibieca was not taken until March 27, 1938; hence during the final year the village was in the Nationalist zone. During the first two years of the war, when Ibieca was in the Republican zone only fifteen miles from the battlefront, the village's experience was conditioned by the war itself and by competition and conflict between rival Republican factions—specifically, between anarchist and communist organizations contending for power on the regional and central levels of government. The anarchists and their socialist allies held sway until the summer of 1937, when communists and their allies gained control of both levels of government.

The militia columns dispatched from coastal cities conquered most of eastern Aragon for the Republic by late July. The principal column that marched across the middle of Huesca province was the Ascaso column, composed of units representing various workers' organizations, the National Confederation of Work (CNT) and the Iberian Anarchist Federation (FAI), and by a Marxist party, the United Marxist Workers' party (POUM). Around midday on July 27 the first contingent of militiamen entered Ibieca, armed, bearded, half-naked in undershirts and shorts, black from the sun and dirt of the journey, and speaking Catalan. It was an invasion, not of foreigners, but certainly of outsiders, strangers. The militiamen raised a red flag in the church, took the village in the name of the Republic, and declared that liberty had arrived and that all villagers were equal. There would be no more rich and poor because the land belonged to everyone. It was time to get rid of the *caciques* and the priests.

The effect of this invasion was immediate. Before the war, leftists and rightists had been about evenly balanced in Ibieca. The left centered around the club affiliated with the Radical Socialists which met in Felipe Bravo's house, and the right centered around the club affiliated with the Spanish Confederation of Independent Rightists (CEDA) which met in Carlos Sierra's house. Under the Second Republic, from 1931 to 1936, political activity had increased and temporary polarizations had occurred around election campaigns, but many villagers considered themselves apolitical. With the coming of the war, however, the village underwent a deep and thorough polarization. Although the numbers were still fairly equally divided, everyone was clearly on one side or the other. A few knew they would be shot if they were caught by opposition forces, some were uncertain about what would happen to them, and everyone was closely related to one faction or the other and so was forced to make choices that became allegiances and alliances.

Those who welcomed the militia columns were known as *rojos* (reds) regardless of their political affiliations before the war, and those who did not welcome the columns were called *fascistas* (fascists), again regardless of previous political affiliation. Before the war there had been CNT unions in a few of the surrounding Somontano villages—in Angüés, Loporzano, Torres de Montes, and Montfloriete—but not in Ibieca. However, perhaps a dozen village men had had significant contact with anarchism, its organizations or ideology, and they provided the nucleus of leadership that reorganized the village society after the militiamen declared a revolution. Villagers distinguished these men from their less militant allies by calling them *rojos perdidos* (zealous reds). Francisco Gómez, a schoolteacher, had studied anarchist writings and called himself an anarchist, as did his two brothers, both cartmakers. Several other village men belonged to CNT unions as workers in Barcelona before the war, and a number of poor and landless men, including Daniel Castillo and Eugenio Clavero, encountered anarchist ideas and activists while working on wheat harvest gangs in the south of the province. A few more village men and women caught the "idea" of anarchist revolution when the war started, but many of those considered *rojos* by their less sympathetic neighbors allied with the anarchists in defense of the Republic and were at best fair-weather friends of the anarchist regime.

Luis Solano fled west the night before militiamen arrived and did not stop until he reached Zaragoza, where he spent the first two years of the war. After declaring the new order, the militiamen seized the village priest and debated all afternoon about whether to shoot him. They finally released him, sending him off in secular clothes with a travel pass to join a relative in Tarrasa who was a member of the militant anarchist organization (FAI). Villagers watched the debate passively, and their responses to the outcome defined which factions they were in, if that was not already clear. Because the militiamen let him go, those on the left concluded that the priest was a good man and deserved to live. Those on the right said he had been released because he had informed on fellow villagers: had he been honest, he would have been shot.

The priest was specifically suspected of betraying the location of the gold and silver cups and plates used in mass. These articles had been hidden before the militiamen arrived, and, not long after the priest was released, they went to Casa Segarra and made the women of the house dig up the treasure from the stable floor with their bare hands. The militiamen, along with the avowed leftists in the village, also went to all the houses and gathered devotional paraphernalia—rosaries, prayerbooks, crosses, and saintly images. They entered the church with mules and pulled the saints down, dragged them out to the central plaza, and piled them up—male on top of female saints—along with family religious artifacts and church and municipal government records, including records of debts and land deeds. In the evening they set fire to the pile. Even for disbelievers and those personally relieved by the burning of the documents, the bonfire was a massive shock to the villagers' sense of social order.

The first group of militiamen left with the church bells (to be melted down for ammunition), all ten pair of village oxen (to be butchered for meat), and some other provisions. Four days later another group arrived and committed acts that convinced villagers that the war was very serious and would be a long one. The new arrivals called for denunciations and got one, of Joaquín Murillo, a devout carpenter who worked for wealthy families. He was denounced by a fellow carpenter who was a leftist and a neighbor. Murillo was taken off to another village and shot ten days later. The militiamen then arrested nine more men, including two of the largest landowners after Solano, Fernando Segarra and Juan Blanco, and a small landholder who was the head hired hand in Casa Solano, Benito Cuevas. Cuevas had stayed on in Solano's house to protect his wife, Pilar Nueno, and children. The men were detained for several weeks, threatened with execution, and finally released unharmed.

As the militia columns moved through the eastern Aragonese countryside, they set up or legitimized committees of leftist supporters to manage production and politics in all the villages. In September representatives from the village committees met and established a formal regional administrative structure, the Council of Aragon. The Council coordinated economic activities throughout the region and connected it to the Republican state apparatus as it reemerged in Barcelona. The anarchist blueprint for production, distribution, and consumption was known as libertarian communism. As a scheme of collectivizing the means of production, assigning work according to ability and distributing food and goods according to need, libertarian communism was similar to other collective schemes. What distinguished the anarchist plan, at least in theory, was the stress on spontaneity, on libertarianism. "Anarchists were committed to building a revolutionary movement that did not coerce members"[2] and a social order in which individuals were their own authorities. Ideally, collectivization would be the free expression of the will of individuals.

In Ibieca most of the collective's advocates were those with few resources—the land-poor and landless—although some larger holders were quite sympathetic. Ibieca's committee was composed of landless workers, poor and small landholders, and artisans, all of whom had been powerless as well as poor until the Second Republic. The collective itself was constituted in the form of a CNT union, which everyone joined, when representatives from the district committee in Angüés came with instructions on forming collectives. At first villagers retained their land, while Solano's estate was divided into lots and distributed among land-poor and landless households, some thirty of the seventy-five in the village. By the time the winter wheat was sown in the late fall, all village land (including garden land) was collectivized, as were all draft animals, livestock, machinery, and tools. Solano's stables and storerooms were converted into a collective warehouse, the church into a granary, Casa Costa into a cooperative store, and Solano's olive mill into the village livery. The committee assigned work tasks, discriminating only in terms of age and sex. The land of the village was worked, the livestock kept, and grapes and olives pressed into wine and olive oil by all able-bodied village men. Luis Segarra, Fernando's son and heir, was assigned to work under Benito Cuevas, Solano's former hired hand, in an inversion of the prewar social hierarchy that probably made both men uncomfortable. Most women's work continued to be done on a household basis as before, except that all servants were dispatched and wealthy women had to work themselves. The major female task that was collectivized was bread-

2. Kaplan, *Anarchists of Andalusia*, p. 206.

making, which poor women saw wealthy women doing for the first time in their lives.

The explicit organizing principle in the village during those months was "From each according to his ability, to each according to his need." Essential food and goods were rationed to households according to number of residents, age, and sex. Everyone was paid for work with coupons (*bonos*), which they exchanged at the village cooperative for unrationed food and goods. The cooperative was run by twelve-year-old Mariano Castillo under the supervision of his father, Daniel, a small landholder and leftist. Money was not used in exchanges between village families, and money confiscated from families by the committee at the beginning of the war was used to purchase certain goods outside the village. For example, the committee bought mules to replace the oxen that had been expropriated. Otherwise, the village committee bartered with the district warehouse in Angüés, exchanging its surpluses for scarce goods and foodstuffs.

Some problems were handled in the village, and others were taken to the district committee in Angüés. Many villages accepted the reorganization of work more readily than the reorganization of consumption. They did not like others exercising control over their access to food, goods, and services, but there was no remedy to the problems as long as they stayed in the collective. Because many were also dissatisfied with collectivized gardening, the village committee petitioned Angüés for permission to revert to private gardening. Permission was granted and garden lots were given out to households, one lot per member. The most serious difficulty villagers experienced involved the continuous levies, confiscations, and outright thefts of food and goods by soldiers. Ibieca was within a day's walk from the front, and as the war went on the levies and the villagers' intolerance of them only increased. People often lodged complaints with the Angüés committee, but little could be done.

Under the anarchist regime there were no Catholic burials, weddings, baptisms, or masses. At burials women sang folksongs, and one couple was married in a civil ceremony—both sins, according to Catholic doctrine. The common greeting, *adiós* (roughly, "God be with you") was prohibited and replaced with *salud* (roughly, "Go in good health"). Juan Blanco worried that a militia captain billeted in his house would denounce the whole family when he found out that Juan's daughter said to her parents each night before she went to sleep, "Good night, until tomorrow, if God is willing."

Name-calling and verbal disputes continued between villagers through the period, and the new rules of etiquette were frequent vehicles for struggle. Angela Iglesias made it a point to say *adiós*, especially to committee members, and then to correct herself, claiming she had forgotten the rule, when they protested and called her a fascist. One day a political commissar, a young man from the area who had attended village fiestas and dances many times before the war, came to make an inspection. He passed by Angela's house, riding in a car with a mounted machine gun. Angela called down to him; he ignored her. Angela called out that she had danced with him often, that in the past he had recognized her and followed behind her, waiting for her attention and inviting her to dance. The commissar responded with a vulgar gesture. Angela went into her house, got a pitcher of water, and tossed it on the commissar. She got away with this and also earned respect from both left and right, because the commissar had violated the code of good conduct between men and women that all villagers shared.

After December, 1936, anarchists gradually lost power in the central government of the Republican zone and in the Council of Aragon, over which they had initially had total control. In August, 1937, the Council was abolished and replaced with a governing structure totally subordinated to the central government and controlled by a coalition of Republicans, Socialists, and Communists. At the same time a decree was issued, specifically directed at Aragon, where the collective movement was strongest, supporting the rights of individual collective members to withdraw and recover their original property.[3]

Collectivization worked economically but depended on control of the political apparatus at the center as well as in municipalities to survive.[4] The ousting of the anarchists from the government and the decree supporting individual production sounded death knells for collectivization, and villagers knew it. The Republicans and the

3. *Boletín Oficial de Aragón*, I, 1, Circular no. 2, August 22, 1937.
4. Borkenau, *Spanish Cockpit*; Jackson, "Living Experience"; Souchy, *Entre los campesinos*; Thomas, "Anarchist Agrarian Collectives."

Casa Iglesias

Angela Iglesias

Communist party sought a kind of state and polity too centralized
to be built on an economic and political foundation of collectives,
which were highly autonomous and decentralized. The new governors of the Republican state were not in a position to abolish the
collectives in August, 1937, but they did harass them, in addition to
encouraging individualized forms of economic activity. Communist
militia units were dispatched to Aragon, particularly to the Ebro
River valley, where the collectivization movement was most powerful, to disrupt and dismantle many CNT unions which operated
collectives. In September, 1937, a new district committee was
formed in Angüés and a contingent of militiamen were sent to sur-

rounding villages, including Ibieca, to demonstrate the shift in power from *collectivistas* to *individualistas* and to ensure that individuals were allowed to withdraw from the collectives. Given the shift in official policy, about half the village withdrew from the collective. By the time the Nationalists took over, most of the previously landed houses had recovered their estates. The collective, composed of landless and some land-poor houses, continued working Solano's estate. It also maintained the cooperative, which was still important, but less so as money replaced coupons and barter between individuals in and among villages.

Before the Nationalists took the village on March 27, 1938, about twenty men and a few families fled east. Most returned before the war was over or shortly thereafter; at least two men were killed, and three sought permanent exile in France. With a few exceptions, the men who returned were arrested and sent to concentration camps. Those who were released before the war was over were conscripted into the Nationalist Army and sent to fight against those they had once supported. In Ibieca the Nationalists levied food and goods from village stocks and called for denunciations. Luis Solano returned while the troops were still there, but he and his wife decided the threat of denunciation was worth more than the fact of it and did not turn in any of their neighbors. Those endangered by Solano's knowledge knew who they were because his family cut off all social contact with them, refusing even to greet them when passing in the street. While Solano recovered his estate and reaped the harvests sown by the collective, he did not recover his former status in the village. The revolution had robbed him of the aura of invulnerability.

The Civil War and anarchist revolution left enduring scars on village lives. A dozen young men died while fighting in one or the other army. One man was executed in Ibieca, another was shot while trying to cross over to the Nationalists, and two were killed while fleeing Nationalist troops. Others sought permanent exile in France, and during the 1940s a few families moved to other cities in Spain because they were unable to live any longer with their neighbors. Anarchists and their allies who stayed or returned after the war lived for years in fear of being denounced, and their memories of collectivization were gradually worn down by the combination of defeat and Franquist propaganda. None of the "reds" still in Ibieca in the 1970s could speak with clarity or ease about their experience.

Anarchist collectivization and rule was a direct and concerted assault on religious authority and belief and on caciqual power and property. The attack tormented many villagers, not only the rich but also poorer villagers who were devoted to wealthier families or to the church and the priest. Sara Segarra, who was in her teens during the war, still shook with anger in the 1970s when she described the anarchists' desecration of the church and their attacks on her father. In her words, "No one ruled here then. Everything belonged to everyone and anyone. The system worked all right, and it was bad, very bad. It did not make us all equal. It made the poor rich and the rich poor." Angela Iglesias's husband, Benito Cuevas, was almost shot for aiding Luis Solano's wife, Pilar, and their children. Soldiers removed religious pictures, statues, literature, and ornaments from her house to burn; they took food and goods even though her family was a poor one; her father died and was buried without Catholic rites, and her mother went insane during the war. Angela and her husband were heckled and harassed as fascists for their enduring loyalty to the Solanos and for their contempt for the anarchists. After the war they, like the Solanos and others so deeply affronted, shunned neighbors who had participated in the anarchist regime.

Juan Blanco, who owned an eighty-five-hectare estate, had been Luis Solano's major ally in political struggles before the war. In late July, 1936, Juan, his wife, and three children fearfully watched from their balcony as members of the Ascaso column poured into Ibieca on the road up from Velillas. His wife and daughter had hidden their family's religious relic, a silver heart of Jesus, in the manure pile, and the troops never found it. Juan was threatened with execution, then confined to his home while his confiscated fields were worked by and for his neighbors. In early 1937 rumors spread that there would be more executions, and Juan fled to the mountains. He joined his brother in Benasque, then crossed the border into France for the duration of the war. In March, 1938, Juan's wife and children watched again from their balcony as troops filed into the village; this time they rejoiced, for it was a day of liberation for them. Juan returned home immediately and, like Luis Solano, resumed his power and property, but not his full authority. The ideological grip of village *caciques* had been eroded somewhat by prewar struggles but was broken by the anarchist inversion of the social order. The rich continued to rule, but, in the eyes of many, they had irrevocably lost the right to rule.

Those who joined in the anarchist experiment and who stayed in Ibieca or returned after the war struggled with the meaning of defeat and the bitterness of their neighbors. The positive experience of effectively reorganizing and running village agriculture for a year was lost in the mire of what had gone wrong. Lorenzo Lobera, who worked in the collective in nearby Angüés during the war, could only recall the experience in negative terms. He said most villagers, himself included, were not "prepared" for the idea of collectivization. Some worked as little as possible because they felt others reaped all benefit from their labor. He also did not like his work and travel being governed by the village committee. Lorenzo believed more passionately in the idea of collectivization at the time, but in light of defeat he stressed the failures, the loss of autonomy and control. No friend of Franco, he said he preferred to "work for myself, not anyone else, to command my own kingdom," his own *casa*.

It was difficult for villagers who had supported collectivization during the war to separate defeat from failure, and more generally to separate the war from the revolution. In part because war and revolution were merged experientially, the literature on the anarchist revolution in Spain is fraught with contradictions and debate. Some observers argue that the collectives were imposed on villagers, not spontaneously generated by them; that collectivization failed as a system of production to supply cities and troops with food; and that the majority of village landowners—the peasantry—opposed the collectives. Others argue that the revolution was a spontaneous response of villages that drew on centuries of oppression and hardship and on the core values of village life; that the collectives were a success productively; and that the difficulties peasants had with the collective regime were imposed by circumstances of war or the result of betrayal by their allies, not rooted in a rejection of libertarian communism.

Those who condemn the collectives point to the circumstances of war, such as the climate of coercion, as if they were part of the collectivization process. Defenders separate the war and collectivization, attributing all the problems and wrongdoings that occurred under the collective regime to the circumstances of war. Clearly, it is a mistake to condemn collectivization for events that invariably come about with war, but conversations with the villagers of Ibieca and firsthand accounts from CNT militants and other Aragonese villagers gathered by Ronald Fraser also recommend that we resist judging the collectives as if they could be distilled from the war.

Wartime collectivization in Spain was a unitary experience. There is truth in all the positions above, for anarchist collectivization in wartime was an intensely and inescapably contradictory experience. Most Aragonese villages contained a nucleus of supporters for the anarchist revolution, and many villagers joined collectives eagerly. The Aragonese collectives were highly successful as measured by crop production, which increased 20 percent over prewar years. On the other hand, many villagers participated unwillingly in collectives and, for all, the climate of coercion created by the executions and threat of executions made real choice impossible. Although food and supplies were sufficient overall, their distribution on all levels created conflicts and problems that were most often resolved by fiat rather than by real consent. Realities such as these took the "libertarian" out of libertarian communism and eventually made it difficult for the most ardent anarchists in the area fully to support collectivization.

Discussions of collectivization and peasant ideology usually center on the peasantry's commitment to autonomy and equality and their hostility toward authority and hierarchy. Obviously the coercive aspects of wartime collectivization contradict these values. What did wartime collectivization as such—as a system of production and distribution—mean to villagers? Did it express the peasant value system or violate it?

Again, the answer seems to be both. Drawing on accounts of village life and anarchist insurrections and activities in Andalusia before the war, Julian Pitt-Rivers and Gerald Brenan have argued that libertarian communism as an ideology was a pure expression of peasant egalitarianism and localism, values which emerged from the experience of subsistence agriculture and village life. According to Jerome Mintz, "anarchosyndicalist principles matched campesino notions of cooperation and the exchange of labor," and "natural" social rules, the village code of conduct and community pressure, would prevail, unfettered in the absence of church and state.[5] The experience of Ibieca and other Aragonese villages supports these arguments to some extent, but also suggests that other values and social relations were not so reinforced and provided the basis for serious discontent with the collective regime.

Land-poor and landless villagers and young men and women were disproportionately represented among the active supporters of collectivization in Ibieca and elsewhere in Aragon. Jaime Avila, the son of a medium landholding peasant in a lower Aragonese village, Mas de las Matas, explained to Ronald Fraser that he had no objection to working for the collective—" 'it's an obligation to work anyway'— and was pleased to have got a new jacket and a pair of trousers from the collective store, something he had not been able to afford before. Nor did he find it unduly strange to work without pay. In a great many farmers' homes sons did not get a wage."[6] Juan Martínez, a medium landholding peasant in Mas de las Matas, who gave up a general store as well as his land under collectivization, nevertheless could see the logic of collectivization as a system of production and as a remedy for the poor: "To work in common is by no means stupid. It meant large concentrations of land instead of small, scattered plots, which saved time and effort. We didn't live worse under collectivization than before—or only to the extent made inevitable by the war. Those who had had less—and there were quite a few of them before—now ate more and better. But no one went short."[7] What bothered Martínez was what bothered Lorenzo Lobera of Ibieca and many other peasant landholders—having to turn over everything they produced to collective stores, "the pile," and getting only rations and coupons in return.

Jaime Avila of Mas de las Matas thought working collectively was better than working alone but said "it was necessary to have a stimulus, a drive—and that was what was missing" from the collective regime. The village schoolmaster, Alfredo Cancer, said that the

---

5. Pitt-Rivers, *People of the Sierra*; Brenan, *Face of Spain*; Mintz, *Casas Viejas*, pp. 80, 129.

6. Fraser, *Blood of Spain*, p. 355.

7. Ibid., p. 361.

poor were much better off under collectivization, for it added olive oil, rice, sausage, and meat to their diet of bread, potatoes, and water. But the peasants did not want to give up what was theirs, and "that was the only reason they favoured the fascists."[8] "It wasn't that the anarchists' ideals were bad—they were simply utopian. I was no property owner and had no reason to be hostile to them out of fear of losing my wealth. Nor was I political. It seems fine that I should teach the shoemaker's son free and the shoemaker should make me a pair of shoes for nothing. But what really happened was a loss of incentive. We Aragonese are independent-minded, freedom-lovers, healthily proud. Without freedom, what is there?"[9] Cancer estimated that over half the collective's members who had been peasant owners felt that they were giving up *their* crops when they turned them over to the collective stores, no matter whose land they had actually worked. The CNT committee president of Mas de las Matas agreed and added that the majority of villagers did not "believe the collectives could work with everything going on 'the pile'; they felt they had to ask for what was theirs by right—it was like having to beg."[10]

The lot of the land-poor and the landless improved considerably under collectivization; they gained food, goods, housing, power, and dignity. So did young people, because collectivization created a sphere beyond parental control in which all who worked were equals. But peasant men and women—the heads of landed *casas*—lost under collectivization in some ways that went beyond the loss of their property. They were primary beneficiaries of the prewar social order of autonomous landed *casas*; the collectivized social order deprived *casa* heads of their control over production, distribution, and consumption, and hence of significant power and authority in their lives. The *casa*'s productive property was stripped away, peasants lost independent control over the productive process, and (apparently most disheartening of all) they lost independent control over the fruits of their labor. In some villages, such as Ibieca, where men and women were paid in coupons for their work, the problem was milder; in other collectives, all food and goods

8. Ibid., p. 356.
9. Ibid., p. 361.
10. Ibid., p. 362.

were rationed to *casas* according to the number, age, and sex of family members. Total rationing eliminated a realm of consumption decisions that were central to the social reality and personal meaning of the *casa*. Control over such decisions was what peasants meant when they described what was missing under collectivization. It was not just some stubborn love of their own land or an inability to work with and for others. Rather, they were missing the stimulus, the drive, to maintain the *casa* and to pass it on to their children. Young people and the poor who lacked estates were more often able to identify with the good of the village collective and its social organization as a rationale for working than were *casa* heads. Collectivization realized in some measure the peasant ideology of village autonomy, but it nullified the autonomy of the *casa*. At least in Aragon, the social identity of the peasant was tied first and foremost to the *casa*, not to the village as a whole.

Nor was the attack on village *caciques* and priests so unambiguous for the Aragonese peasantry. In the discussions of Brenan and Pitt-Rivers, *caciques* and priests are portrayed as natural objects of hatred for Andalusian peasants and day laborers, who saw them as outsiders and exploiters. Pitt-Rivers and Brenan argue that anarchist ideology tapped this natural hatred by marking the rich, the church, and the state for violent overthrow. However, a close reading of accounts of arrests and executions in Aragon at the beginning of the war does not indicate they were either straightforward expressions of class hatred or serious expressions of the anarchist revolutionary project.

The militiamen from Catalonia were bent on conquest and securing their rearguard. They spoke of revolutionary ideals when they called for denunciations, but they conducted no investigations, formal hearings, or trials that conveyed their concepts of justice. Only when influential leftists intervened and contradicted a denunciation might someone be released. Joaquín Murillo's execution in Ibieca had little to do with either war or revolution, according to one of his neighbors, who said that Murillo was denounced by a fellow carpenter out of rivalry. In Mas de las Matas, the brother of an executed man said that the executions were caused not by politics but by personal hatreds, vendettas, and envy. Of course, hatreds based on class conflicts are always experienced as personal hatreds;

the point here is that there was no systematic effort to explore a denunciation, to pursue only the charges stemming from injustice as defined by the new egalitarian social order, and to use the judicial process to define and legitimize the new social order.

Had there been such an effort, many villagers in Aragon would still have abhorred it. While the execution, exile, and expropriation of *amos* and priests during the war did free and relieve villagers, many were traumatized by the extremity of measures taken against the wealthy and devout. Especially in small villages such as Ibieca, where peasants predominated, resentment against *caciques* and priests was mitigated by bonds of neighborhood and day-to-day relations of work and devotion. Solano, Blanco, and Segarra were not outsiders by any means, and even the priest, though an outsider, was not considered an intruder by most villagers. If anything, the militiamen were the ones who were resented as outsiders, speaking Catalan and orchestrating arrests, requisitions, and the desecration of sacred objects. The *caciques* and the priest presided over two village-wide authority systems, the *caciques* linking up mainly men through economic and political bonds, and the priest prevailing over mostly women through their devotion to the Virgin Mary and through religious rites. These hierarchical relations contradicted the egalitarianism and individualism of peasant men in particular, but their violent suppression was far more disturbing to the social and symbolic peace of the village than the contradictions had been.

The militiamen who triggered the revolution in Aragon were not carrying out a well-laid plan. The organization and chain of command of the columns was still unsettled when they set out to take the Catalan and Aragonese countryside in August, 1936. Groups of militiamen acted in relation to understandings of the war and revolution that they had formed as workers in large cities and as members of anarchist and socialist unions. No one had any extensive experience with the practice of libertarian communism. No less than the propaganda delegate on the Council of Aragon, the anarchist Juan Zafón, said to Ronald Fraser, "We were attempting to put into practice a libertarian communism about which, it is sad to say, none of us really knew anything." Because of lack of experience and the pressure of expediency wrought by war, militants found themselves making a revolution that even they themselves did not want. The secretary of the Mas de las Matas collective, a CNT member who was deeply committed to anarchist principles and to his village, told Fraser as he described the collective distribution system, "Without even realizing it we had created an economic dictatorship!"[11]

All this might boil down to saying that war is hell and a revolution is not a tea party, were it not for the commitment to "spontaneity" in anarchist ideology. In the anarchist vision, consent was essential to the definition of libertarian communism, in both its genesis and its outcome. As a result of the Civil War experience, many anarchists abandoned the idea that the anarchist vision could be achieved through armed insurrection or revolution. As Macario Royo, an Aragonese CNT leader, put it in a conversation with Ronald Fraser: "To establish libertarian communism means making the revolution; revolutions are made only by force. Everything that is imposed by force has to be maintained by force. The outcome may be communism but it isn't libertarian. . . . Libertarian communism could be established only if the majority of the people already supported communism and then started to organize that communism *freely*."[12] Royo went beyond saying that the Civil War contaminated the anarchist revolution with coercive realities; *all* revolutions are coercive, hence nonlibertarian. Libertarian communism must evolve among people who choose it. Even this position is thorny. Royo's statement ends with an unasked question: What happens to the minority who do not choose libertarian communism?

Dilemmas such as these, plus the extraordinary revolutionary zeal of anarchists before they were chastened by war, have led many observers to interpret and portray anarchist revolts as outbursts of millenarian sentiment among Spain's peasants and rural poor.[13] My reconstruction of events in Ibieca, like Fraser's reconstruction of revolutionary events in other Spanish villages, does not square with such an interpretation. Instead, it lends further credence to the al-

---

11. Ibid., pp. 349–50 n. 1.
12. Ibid.
13. Hobsbawm, *Primitive Rebels*, makes the classic case. See critiques by Kaplan, *Anarchists of Andalusia*, pp. 206–12, and Mintz, *Anarchists of Casas Viejas*, pp. 271–76.

ternative interpretive approach developed by Temma Kaplan and Jerome Mintz in their accounts of anarchism in Andalusia before the Civil War. Kaplan and Mintz agree that anarchist protests, strikes, and insurrections did not represent upwellings of irrational, prepolitical fury; rather, they were the outcome of sustained organizational and ideological efforts, on the one hand, and of historically specific events that escalated the actions of particular groups, on the other hand. In some Aragonese villages, such as Ibieca, where the organizational and ideological groundwork was weak, historical events played the major role. In cities along the northeastern coast of Spain, when the Republican state collapsed in the wake of Franco's coup, highly mobilized, predominantly anarchist militant organizations rushed into the breach and took command, first of the cities, and then of the surrounding countryside. The revolution in the countryside was foremost a response to this circumstance, to the transfer of effective state power from the Republicans to the anarchists, which signaled the inversion of the social order. The new order, libertarian communism, tapped some village values. It was not, however, the natural distillate of the rural ethos of the region, but the collective vision of an anarchist movement with a fifty-year history in Spain and with urban (even international) as well as rural sources.

The millenarian interpretation of anarchism in Spain is not based on careful scrutiny of organizations and events so much as it is an elaboration of popular assumptions about anarchism that cast it as the antithesis of order, the enemy of organization. Events in Ibieca, and in other villages, towns, and cities that participated in the anarchist revolution during the Spanish Civil War, dramatically refute such assumptions. With remarkable speed, anarchists generated a new order and new organizations in place of the ones they overthrew. In Ibieca private property, wage labor, household labor, and monied exchanges were replaced by a collective and a cooperative that effectively produced crops and distributed goods and services and that were linked into a district and regional system of economic administration and exchange. The anarchist economy was organized; so was the polity. Governing councils existed in each village, district committees handled problems that could not be settled locally, and the region was presided over by a council of elected representatives from the political parties.

Certainly there was order and organization to anarchism. Moreover, Royo's reservations aside, it is at least conceivable that the anarchist revolution could have succeeded in Spain had larger historical events moved with the anarchists instead of against them— had they maintained state power, won the war, and been blessed with a healthy economy and powerful international allies. Still, the revolutionary experience in Aragon and in Ibieca revealed a problem, more ideological than organizational, that would have afflicted an anarchist regime no matter how auspicious the circumstances.

The contradiction between anarchist ideas of individual freedom and collective order would have been troubling for libertarian communism anywhere, even if it had been arrived at in a climate free from terror and if all had joined the collectives voluntarily. However, in Aragon, where individual freedom and *casa* autonomy were culturally merged, the tension between the two values was powerfully disillusioning because the collective order virtually dissolved the *casa* as a unit of decisionmaking about production, distribution, and consumption. In Ibieca and other Aragonese villages, we have seen that especially *casa* heads—the majority of adults in most villages—lost their sense of drive and the stimulus for work under collectivization. More "preparation" and better administration would have helped ease the tension, perhaps, but would not have eliminated the contradiction. Given the cultural identification of *casa* autonomy and personal freedom in Aragon, the "communism" in libertarian communism would have had to give more rein to *casas*, lest the "libertarian" be sacrificed.

The prewar social order was reimposed as swiftly as the anarchists had overthrown it. It began to resurface after the anarchists lost power in the regional council of Aragon in August, 1937, and was fully restored when Nationalist troops recaptured the Somontano in March, 1938. The village was deeply traumatized by the experience of war or revolution,[14] but the underlying social and cultural structures of *caciquismo*, the church, *amo*/labor relations, and peasant *casas* survived and recovered. Aside from deaths, injuries, and irreparable material losses, probably the major enduring effects of the war and revolution were broken relations, bitter feelings, and

14. Erikson, *Everything in Its Path*, describes the symptoms of a community so extremely traumatized by a disaster that it seemed unable to reconstitute itself socially.

a loss of a sense of invulnerability, and perhaps of legitimacy, on the part of those who commanded the social hierarchies.

Although Francisco Franco came to power in defense of these social hierarchies, within a decade his regime inaugurated a program of agrarian reforms that would unmake the old social order of *caciquismo*, the church, preindustrial capitalist agriculture, and peasant *casas* as radically as had the anarchists. We shall see that critical differences contributed to the success of the Franco agrarian reform: it did not invert the class structure; it was slower and surreptitious; and it was *casa* centered, the outcome of individual choices, not an explicit plan. Before unraveling the events and processes by which the men and women of Ibieca remade their village under Franco, let us examine in more detail the social order which survived until midcentury.

❋ Chapter Three
❋ *Ibieca before the*
❋ *Franco Reforms*

The social world of Ibieca before the Franco reforms combined three interpenetrating realms of social relations: two realms of productive relations, and a third of social reproduction. The organization of agricultural work on large estates generated a hierarchical realm of relations between the families of *amos* and agricultural and domestic workers, while the social relations of production on smaller estates generated peasant egalitarianism. The realms overlapped, in that many peasant families also relied on wage work on large estates, and others on occasion hired wage laborers themselves. The social reproduction and continuity of the third realm, the *casa*--the union of family (living, deceased, and not yet born) and house, land, and animals—was the common goal of both forms of production. All three realms set up lines of autonomy and dependence that divided villagers in some ways and in other ways served as the sources of coherence and connectedness of village society.

Material and Social Connections

The following sections explore the three social realms of old Ibieca by surveying the lines of autonomy and dependence in their material, political, economic, and familial manifestations.

Families, Land, and Animals

In old Ibieca the material exchanges, the ecological cycles, were largely local. Much of what went into Ibieca's houses came from the land, and much of what issued from village houses was returned to the land. The *casa* was a miniature ecosystem. The degree of self-sufficiency varied greatly from large landholding to poor landholding houses, but the *casa* at each extreme defined a bounded system within which primary material exchanges occurred.

Ibieca's water returned to the land that issued it. The village fountain drew water from an underground stream through five iron pipes. Villagers filled jugs, pails, and barrels from the pipes for household use; the runoff flowed into a trough used to water work animals, and then into a large square stone basin where women washed clothes. The runoff from the washbasin was channeled into an irrigation system, which in turn channeled the water through the village gardens.

Three parallel irrigation canals, two of them fed by the washbasin and one by another spring, defined three sections of gardens in a small valley that ran south of the fountain. Each section was cut into a series of steps. The combined effect was a patchwork of lush greens, the patches at different levels, stepping down the slope from the fountain. The garden land (*huerta*) consisted of only about two hectares but was crucial to household subsistence. The valley steps were divided into garden plots; each household owned one or two gardens. A wide variety of vegetables were cultivated for both human and animal consumption. Potatoes, several kinds of beans, onions, and tomatoes were most important. There were a half-dozen kinds of fruit trees, including apple, pear, and fig, and a dozen kinds of flowers. The gardens also produced more or less wild blackberries, snails, and cane, the latter used in making baskets and chair seats.

Except for a few very small plots, the rest of village land was unirrigated (*secano*). Like the garden steps, its small plains and gentle slopes were divided into plots owned by households. The steeper slopes and more rugged terrain—about half of the village territory— was not cultivated or marked off by household boundaries, though most of it was privately owned. The land of even the poorest owners was broken into dozens of scattered parcels. The fragmentation of holdings may ultimately derive from historical patterns of pioneering, pawning, and auctioning of land in small lots. However, the practice made ecological sense, too, as it provided protection against microclimatic vagaries. Frosts, for example, often damaged crops more in one part of the territory than in another.

In 1950 the cultivated land was a patchwork of cereal fields, olive

Washing clothes at the washbasin

Vegetable garden plots

and almond groves, and vineyards—nearly eight hundred plots in all. From their harvests of barley, oats, and wheat families reserved one-fifth as seed for the following year; the rest was either ground into feed or flour, or marketed. Household harvests of olives were pressed into olive oil, and harvests of grapes into wine. Most landed houses produced just enough to meet their needs for the following year or two. Those with surpluses sold them to muleteers or to merchants from nearby towns and cities who came through the village regularly after the harvests. The uncultivated half of village territory was either utterly barren, covered with low-growing scrub oak (*carascal*) or cleared of brush and bushes for pasturing livestock. Scrub oak trees were an important resource, furnishing village homes with firewood and providing acorns that were gathered to feed the pigs.

The wealth and status of a house was indicated directly by the number of draft animals it possessed; some houses had none, most had at least one, and a few had several pair. Until the 1920s all these beasts (*la dula*) were taken out once a day by a special herder (*el dulero*) to pasture on common lands. In 1950 there were still about eighty work animals in Ibieca, and at watering time early in the morning and late in the day there was a veritable stampede down to the fountain. In prior decades goats had been kept for cheese and skins, but by 1950 only a few remained in village flocks to nurse the lambs of dry ewes. The main contribution of sheep to village families was wool, which was made into yarn and cloth and used to stuff mattresses. Except on rare occasions, neither goats nor sheep were slaughtered for meat. Small animals raised in first-floor stables—chickens, rabbits, hens, and pigs—supplied villagers with meat for holidays and periods of most arduous labor.

A list of the food, goods, and services that Ibieca's landed families drew from their gardens, orchards, fields, and livestock would include the following:

cereals (bread, feed)
grapes (wine)
olives (cooking oil, lamp fuel)
vegetables
fruit
flowers

cane (baskets, chairs)
hemp (linen)
carascal (firewood, charcoal, acorns)
earth (construction materials)
water (drinking, irrigation, washing)
burros, mules, oxen (transport, plowing)
sheep (wool, skins, meat)
goats (milk, cheese, skins)
rabbits, chickens, pigs, pigeons, hens (meat, eggs)
cats and dogs (hunt mice and game)

Almonds, animal skins, and surplus cereals, wine, olive oil, wool, and other foodstuffs were marketed. The larger the landholding, the greater the market involvement. Marketing, however, did not compromise the powerful sense of autonomy generated by village households producing most of what they consumed and consuming much of what they produced.

So comprehensive were the material cycles in old Ibieca that there was almost no material waste. Every almond, olive, and grape was picked each year, and cereal grains left in the fields or spilled on the road after the harvest were recovered. The only land truly unused was that covered with rocky outcrops. Every piece of the slaughtered pig was made into food, and villagers picked clean all bones, including skulls, of all animals. Outside an occasional scrap thrown them, cats survived on rats and mice, which was the service that justified their existence. Scraps were fed more regularly to donkeys and dogs. Donkeys returned something to villagers in the form of transport, dogs in hunting, and both in companionship. Animal and human excrement was faithfully accumulated and transformed into manure for next year's crops. When something really was thrown away—a broken pot that could not be repaired or a worn-out strap that could not be mended—it was tossed on the village outskirts, in the buffer zone between family and field, where villagers gradually lost sight of it.

Villagers were intimately dependent on the immediate world around them, and they knew that world extensively and intensively. Their knowledge of other distant and unrelated worlds was scanty. Huesca was the closest other world to Ibieca, and it was three-and-a-half hours away if one walked swiftly. Until about 1950, when radios became common, most village homes relied exclusively on word of mouth for news. By the time a news item arrived in Ibieca, it had been reshaped and crafted by the messenger into something that would be meaningful to local lives. The world of the village was so much more powerful and compelling that it shaped the villagers' experience of all other realities. The land, animals, and the elements were creatures in villagers' social world—people named them, knew them intimately, and were attached to them emotionally. The winds were named and distinguished by their direction, their relative temperature, and their chances of carrying rain. Every parcel of land owned in the village territory was named, and men knew how each of theirs would fare given different combinations of crops and weather conditions. Women knew the uncultivated margins and slopes more intimately, the places where medicinal plants, herbs, and wildflowers grew.

Ecologically, the landed *casas* of Ibieca were universes of interdependencies among family, land, animals, and the elements. The immanent experience of each *casa's* material universe relative to others was one of autonomy, self-governance, and self-sufficiency.

Reciprocal Exchanges, Wage Work, and Commerce

Old Ibieca was also a world of unlike units, or unlike groups of households, that relied on each other's labor, services, and goods. All landed houses were more self-sufficient than landless houses, but only medium landholding houses operated largely outside the wage-labor exchanges. Houses with large landholdings engaged numerous temporary and some permanent workers, both agricultural and domestic, while small and poor landholding houses—the majority of the landed houses—and most of the landless houses hired out one or more of their members on a temporary or permanent basis.

Peasant families, in spite of their relative self-sufficiency, cultivated networks of kin, neighbors, and friends whom they could call on for labor, and to some extent for food and goods, in both generalized and balanced reciprocal exchanges.[1] The most common pat-

1. See Brandes, *Migration, Kinship and Community*, ch. 5, and Freeman, *Neighbors*, pp. 145–46, for descriptions of labor exchanges in other Spanish villages.

terns were for two families to share a team of work animals (*yuntero*) or a small machine, or to pool human labor on a regular basis. The arrangement that Eugenio Clavero made after the Civil War was typical. His daughter's family moved to Sesa to rent and run a brick factory for fifteen years, and Eugenio stayed home alone, working out a labor-sharing arrangement with Casa Abad next door. They had more land than Eugenio, and Eugenio needed a place to board; so they arranged to work each other's lands jointly, and Eugenio boarded in Casa Abad. It was a neighborly arrangement in which no money changed hands.

Sharing resources with neighbors and kin was a major survival strategy of peasant households that cushioned them from hardships. Sharing also created or fortified social bonds that were an end in themselves and that could serve other ends. Through his arrangement with Casa Abad, Eugenio Clavero gained something of a family. Like *amo*/laborer arrangements, a sharing arrangement was renewed each year or it lapsed. Most arrangements did not last more than a few years, but some, such as the mulesharing and migrant harvesting arrangements between Casa Miranda and Casa Gavín, were passed down from parents to children.

Arrangements to share productive resources and labor were usually explicit and were made by the male heads of households. Women also pooled resources on a more informal basis, helping each other with gardening, cooking, and cleaning chores in times of family crisis, such as illness and death. Each year a small network of women joined to make *mondongo* together. After the pig was slaughtered in each woman's house her closest kin, neighbors, and friends would join her in her kitchen for the day to make sweetbreads and sausage. The atmosphere was festive, often ribald, as the women entertained one another telling stories, both true and fictive. Men's close networks were also activated on the day of the pig slaughter. The men held the pig on a metal rack while the butcher slit its throat; then they burned off its hair with flaming scrub-oak branches, washed the carcass, and lifted it onto a metal hook in the corral to be cut up. The men who helped were usually spouses or brothers of the women helping out in the kitchen and were often themselves involved in sharing productive resources. The pig-owning family gave the families who helped them gifts

The Lacasa family slaughtering a pig

(*presentes*) of sweetbreads and cured meats. Women gave gifts in reciprocal exchanges with other families and as payments and favors, calculating them months in advance of the actual kill.

Several more formalized collective arrangements engaged a dozen or more village households. Thirty families owned sheep in the communal flock in 1950. The Society of Livestock Owners of Ibieca hired shepherds, and families paid and boarded them according to how many sheep they owned. The sheep were pastured on the owners' fallow and pasture land as a flock during the day and divided up at night to sleep in their owners' stables. Until 1952 there was, in addition to Solano's olive oil mill, a mill owned by a dozen families

After a day of making mondongo

that processed the olives of most village houses, paying its workers
and maintenance costs in kind. Before the Lacasa brothers built a
commercial oven in the late 1940s, women baked their bread in the
village oven, again paying the oven workers in kind. Each year the
right to run the oven was auctioned in the plaza to the two highest
bidding houses, who in effect paid the oven's rent for the village to
the municipal government. A woman from each of those houses,
usually one who was young and unmarried, built the oven fire several days a week for the following year and baked the loaves that
village women prepared in their homes. The oven workers were paid

one loaf of bread for every six they baked. The bread earned by the *orneras* more than compensated for the rent paid by their families to the municipal government, so running the oven was a source of income. When Sara Segarra ran the oven during the 1940s her father paid her for the loaves she brought home, and she used the money to buy a sewing machine to prepare her trousseau.

Given the tendency of peasant households toward self-sufficiency and autonomy, supplemented by these arrangements to share resources, why did peasants work for *amos*? The wages were important but probably not necessary for survival, at least for some *casas*. The answer lies in the larger social context of the *amo*/laborer relationship. Laborers ate meals in the *amo*'s house as part of the exchange for labor, and hired hands slept there, usually in the stables. They formed social relationships with their *amo*'s family, relationships that were valuable to small landowners because they needed various nonmonetary rights and services, either during crises or just to get by as peasants. A small landowner's family labor supply expanded and contracted over decades in a domestic cycle, which meant that some years it had a chronic surplus which *amos* could employ. Also, customs of impartible inheritance passed estates on to one child, and unless there were other economic options in the area, non-inheriting offspring either had to be supported fully within the heir's household, marry into another house, or move out of the area. Work in an *amo*'s house enabled an heir to maintain a sibling at home to supplement the household labor pool. Moreover, in working for an *amo*, a laborer was in a position to recommend or hear about work for other kin and friends. In effect, peasants used their laboring relationship with an *amo* to underwrite their position as peasants.

Laborers were also in line for an array of services, favors, and loans. Large landholders owned the machinery for pressing grapes into wine, and they made arrangements with laborers to press their grapes, both those produced by a laborer on his own land and those he received in exchange for harvesting the large owner's grapes. Solano and the owners of the collective olive oil mill milled their workers' olives in exchange for labor. Also, laborers could ask their bosses for favors or influence with respect to outside structures: the exemption of a son from military service, a passport to South

America, or a recommendation for a job, a school, a seminary. Finally, *amos* lent workers money (albeit at high interest rates) in cash, in seed grain, and in mortgages.

Most minifundia and landless families depended on wage work for their livelihoods, but small estate owners also cultivated *amo*/laborer and sharecropping relations as one among several strategies for survival and upward mobility. Occasionally laborers and their families developed long-term relations with their *amos*, but in the Somontano the connection customarily was loose and flexible. Laborers were honor bound to an *amo* for only one year and were free to leave without reprisal each Saint Michael's Day. Given the labor situation in this century at least, a worker with a good reputation could always find a job.

Households also supplemented their incomes by sending daughters to be domestic servants (*crías, muchachas, servientas*) in other houses. In addition to room and board, servants were paid an annual wage. In 1950 a hired hand earned 3,500 to 4,000 pesetas a year, while a domestic servant earned 1,000 to 1,500 pesetas. At what age a girl was sent out to serve varied with the financial and labor needs of a household; generally girls were sent out at eight or ten from very poor houses, and at twelve or fourteen from *casas* with more land. Poorer girls sometimes kept serving after they married, even for the rest of their lives, while others usually stopped serving when they married.

Girls and women served in medium and large landholding houses in Ibieca, other Somontano villages, and Huesca capital. Outside Ibieca families and the girls themselves heard of jobs through other village girls who were doing domestic service and from village boys and men doing agricultural labor. Like the hired hands, domestic servants were hired from one Saint Michael's Day to the next, but the girl's parents were more involved in making the arrangements with the hiring family. Parents had the customary right to children's wages until they married, but generally only the heir designate's wages were pooled with parents' incomes until he or she married. When they could afford to, parents let the other children keep their wages, or saved their wages for them as dowries.

Before 1950 virtually all young women from poorer houses in Ibieca and the Somontano worked as domestic servants for at least a few years before they married. Domestic service for young women was as common as was agricultural wage work for men. Again, it was not simply a matter of material need. A family with a modest landholding might hire a domestic servant even as they sent their own daughter to serve in another house. Domestic service created social connections between families; lateral connections were valued, as well as vertical ones. The daughters themselves also wanted the opportunity to work away from home, to meet people, perhaps to find a better job, to make friends of equal and higher standing, or to find a husband.

Domestic service and agricultural wage work interlaced the lives of rich and poor in old Ibieca. Poorer men and women adopted varying strategies of linking to richer families, but linkages of some kind were inescapable. Some, like Eugenio Clavero, preferred to shift obligations every few years, while others, like Benito Cuevas, continued working for the same family for decades. The stories of Benito and his wife, Angela Iglesias, show us the contours of their family's long-standing relationship with the Solanos and the complexity of Angela's attitude toward the relationship. Their stories also portray the creation of a *casa* in Ibieca and the evolution of its family from 1890 to 1950.

Angela and I spent many hours sitting by the fireplace in her kitchen, talking about her family and her experiences in Ibieca. In the summertime we sat and talked on the old wooden high-backed benches that jut out on each side of the hearth; in the winter we sat on the stone footrests nearer the fire, which was the only source of heat in the house. When I roomed in Angela's house in the early 1970s she lived alone, but in the years before and after the war her house had brimmed with her parents, her husband, and six children.

Angela's parents, both born to poor families in Ibieca, were casado solteros—*they married without so much as knives and forks in their dowries. In the 1890s, with money saved from wage work, they bought a piece of land and built a house on the road to Liesa. Gradually they bought a few orchards and fields and built up a small patrimony. Five of their seven children died before the age of three. Angela and a younger sister were born around 1900; their* parents adopted a third daughter, Rosario, an illegitimate child given up for adoption in Torres de Montes. The child's father, who was from a wealthy family, paid Angela's parents a stipend each month and later paid for Rosario's education as a schoolteacher. Angela and her sister accumulated small dowries by doing wage work and piecework. They both married in the early 1920s, her sister to the heir of a casa in Coscullano, and Angela, who inherited her parents' casa, to Benito Cuevas.

Benito was born in Novales and met Angela in 1917, when he came to Ibieca to work as a hired hand in Casa Solano. He worked in Casa Solano for the rest of his life, with the exception of one year when he went to Jaca to work as a shepherd for one of Luis Solano's cousins. Angela's father also labored for Casa Solano on a daily basis. He and Benito worked their own land and two small estates they sharecropped by lantern light after dark and on Sundays, saving enough money to buy a few more fields. Angela's father also made a carta de gracia contract with a large landowner in Arbaniés who needed several thousand pesetas for his daughter's dowry, loaning him the money in exchange for the use of two small fields on the edge of Ibieca's territory. When the owner could not repay the loan when it was due, he forfeited the field.

The Civil War and postwar years were difficult for Benito and Angela. Angela's father died during the war, and her mother went mad and died shortly thereafter. The burden was lightened as their daughters grew old enough to help Angela and as Ismael, their oldest son, began to join his father in the fields. Ismael worked occasionally in Casa Solano at first, then was hired as a year-round field hand in 1950. Ismael and Benito worked the land they owned and sharecropped after dark and on Sundays, as Benito and his father-in-law had, and in 1953 they made an arrangement that lasted ten years to reap cereals jointly with Casa Barraca. Casa Barraca was a larger estate and the family owned small reaping and winnowing machines, while Casa Iglesias had hands to spare.

As they entered their teens all of Angela's children lived with other families or contributed to their own family's sustenance. María, the oldest child, was informally adopted by Benito's cousin and his wife, who lived around the corner and had no children of their own. The second daughter went to live and serve in Casa

Blanco while in her early teens and stayed there until she married fifteen years later. Ismael's younger brother helped Ismael and their father as he grew old enough. One of his younger sisters went to serve in a wealthy house in Sietamo, while the other did piecework at home for a shop in Huesca.

Angela's family was one of two or three families in Ibieca whose lives were intertwined with the Solano family for several successive generations. Her father, husband, and oldest son worked for the Solanos over a period of eighty years. Angela remembered being generally awestruck by the wealthy when she was a girl, and she used to cry with fear when her mother sent her to Casa Solano to buy meat or milk for a fiesta meal. She said that low-ranking families (la parte baja) looked on high-ranking families (la parte alta) as if they were lordly, even sacred. During the war Angela was shocked at the way the Solanos were treated, and Benito risked his life to protect them. Yet Angela's attitude toward the Solanos was, at least by the 1970s, far from deferential. The Solanos had not maintained Angela's respect over the years; they had not lived up to her expectations for high-ranking families.

Angela said that neither the Solanos nor other wealthy families in Ibieca ever did much for the village as a whole. The only thing she could recall was that they bought statues of saints for the church to replace the ones burned during the Civil War. Despite all their years of service to them, the Solanos never did much for her family, either. Benito died of a lung ailment he contracted while sleeping in the Solano stable with the mules for many winters when he was younger. When Benito and Angela's family used the Solanos' equipment, they paid the same fees as did other families. Neither Luis nor Juan Solano provided her children with any of their contacts for jobs, which instead had come from neighbors and from friends of children. The only favor she could remember one of the Solanos doing for them was when Luis's wife visited Angela's mother on her deathbed and brought them a gift of meat and milk on the day she died.

Angela's relationship to the Solanos did not oblige her to speak or act always in their interest. One morning Angela and I went to Casa Solano to buy surplus onions from its garden. Pedro, an employee of Solano's who was a lifelong friend of Angela's husband, was weighing out the onions in front of the house. Although we all saw that Pedro weighed out twenty kilograms of onions for Angela, he told her to go in the house and pay Solano's wife for twelve kilograms. When I pointed this out to Angela on the way home she brushed it aside, saying Pedro was an old friend of her husband's. From Solano's point of view, Angela and Pedro stole eight kilograms of onions; from Angela's point of view, she had simply taken a gift from Pedro.

Benito's courageous loyalty to Luis Solano's family during the war seems to contradict Angela's present attitude. Partly, things have changed since the war. Angela said the rich stopped lording over Ibieca during the war, and that since then it seems that the poor have become sharper and quicker and the rich duller and denser. No doubt Angela's more recent attitude was affected by the anarchist revolution, which robbed the rich of their prestige, and by their inability to recover it under Franco. Partly, too, her recent attitude, compared with her family's loyalty during the war, reflects the dual value system that the disadvantaged invariably juggle in their relations with the privileged.[2] Angela's detachment and contempt represent the collective consciousness that she and her peers developed through their experience of being exploited. For Angela, at least during the war, that consciousness was subordinated to the hierarchical consciousness that had evolved in her relations with the Solanos. It was one thing to take extra onions from Solano; it had been quite another to take his garden, his fields and orchards, his livestock and his house, as the anarchists had. One act affirmed her values; the other had violated it.

2. Martínez-Alier, *Labourers and Landowners*, has an excellent discussion of the complexity of values available to workers in their relations to bosses in the southern Spanish province of Cordoba: "One should not simply *assume* that the 'social system' exists on a consensus of values from which conduct derives which is compatible with and contributes to the maintenance of the 'social system.' As it has often been said, whether a particular society works like this or not has to be investigated; it cannot be taken for granted. One cannot explain all values as imposed by the system. Andalusian labourers choose conduct which is compatible with the maintenance of *latifundismo* and the social structure based on it; but they have also values which *would* result in conduct incompatible with its maintenance. If they do not adopt these forms of conduct, it is because of controls, which are not social sanctions derived from the agro-town's value system, but rather political controls exercised from the provincial capital and from Madrid" (pp. 314–15).

During the early twentieth century about a quarter of Ibieca's houses were landless except for garden plots. Their lot was poor, sometimes miserable, because they were first and hardest hit by any downswing in agricultural activity. Although some rented and sharecropped patrimonies and fields and so functioned fairly self-sufficiently in the village ecology, their margin of survival was narrowed by the landowner's due. Households that did not own, rent, or sharecrop enough land to be somewhat self-sufficient depended in various ways on those that were, and on the village as a whole. Landless households had rights to gather resources from village common lands. The rights to gather acorns, to collect wood, and to pasture whatever animals they owned were perhaps the most important. They also had gleaning rights (*espigar*) to gather fallen grains from fields and roads after harvesting was over. Otherwise the landless, and poor landholders as well, worked, borrowed, and begged to get by.

The poorest houses without land were those of day laborers (*jornaleros*), who worked on call for large landholding houses on a day-to-day basis. Day laborers were unemployed or underemployed throughout most of the year. During good harvests they were fully or overemployed. When harvests were bad—and rare was the year when all the harvests were good—*jornaleros* were hit hardest because they had no stores from the previous year. During harvest seasons both men and women worked in the fields for wages, or, when a man was being paid per unit harvested, his wife worked with him for nothing to raise his output. Some village men also followed the cereal harvest from south to north into the mountains, until the grape harvest at home was due.

A few occupations were full-time and provided regular income: bricklayer, carpenter, cartmaker, blacksmith, mattressmaker, barber, seamstress, and tailor. The only professionals in Ibieca were the schoolteacher, the priest, and the paramedic (*practicante*)—hardly the makings of a real professional elite. Other professionals, such as a doctor, veterinarian, lawyer, and notary, were two walking hours away, in Angüés. Professionals, permanent workers, and artisans were the "well off" among those without cropland. Many were poor, but some were probably better off than small landholders.

Finally, numerous little trades, skills, and enterprises practiced by the landless and small landholders, and even by the well-to-do, provided occasional income—for example, sheepshearing, tree and vine pruning, beekeeping, and distilling. Some men specialized in transporting crops and goods for others, and others traded goods and crops between villagers and Huesca and the mountains. One family made linen and several made stockings on a piecework basis. Full-time cafes and food stores were established after 1920, but small ones operated in the patios of houses before then.

Entrepreneurialism—activity intended to turn a profit—was widespread in old Ibieca but was encompassed by the social relations of agrarian production. All landed families engaged in some commerce, if only selling their crops and livestock. Most families also engaged in some small enterprise or trade such as making cloth or baskets, pruning trees, or shearing sheep. Some trades and commercial activities took family members away from the village for days and weeks at a time, and some took whole families away for years. Sheepshearers and mattressmakers walked from village to village in the central Somontano each year plying their trades. Lorenzo Lobera learned brickmaking from his father and uncle, who had learned it from their father. When Lorenzo was eight, his parents moved to Angüés, where they first rented a brick factory and then bought one of their own, plus a house and land. In 1942 Lorenzo married Antonia Clavero, Eugenio's daughter, and moved back to Ibieca for five years. Then he moved with his wife and children to Sesa, where he rented and ran another brick factory for fifteen years. When Eugenio's legs "gave out" in 1961 and he could no longer support himself, Lorenzo's family returned to Ibieca and settled into working their patrimony and bringing in wages.

In some instances, or in certain phases of a family cycle of several generations, trades and commerce provided more income than did agriculture, but the enterprises did not transform the *casa*. Rather, the *casa* transformed the income from such enterprises into land, livestock, and dowries. A number of the village *casas* in Ibieca in the 1970s were started by couples who married penniless and generated patrimonies and houses through enterprise. Carlos Bandrés and his son, for example, built up a modestly wealthy *casa* from muleteering during the nineteenth century. Trades, commerce, and skills were usually passed on from father to son, from mother to daughter, but not always. When they were forsaken, the landed houses that had digested the entrepreneurial incomes endured.

The economic and political interdependencies among *casas* created the universe of the village, a whole composed of poor working for rich, of peasants sharing labor and resources, and of all peddling some measure of food, goods, trades, and skills. The experience of the village was dominated by the social relations of the two forms of production, peasant and *amo*/laborer, which generated contradictory images of the whole and potentially conflicting principles of solidarity, one egalitarian and the other hierarchical.

The Casa, *Inheritance, and Marriage*

The Aragonese medieval family law code, the *Derecho Aragones*, continued to govern matters of marriage and inheritance through the Franco regime.[3] According to the code and to custom, inheritance in Aragon was impartible. The house, its furnishings, livestock, and family fields and orchards were passed on to a single heir, the oldest son being preferred. Often enough there were no sons, and occasionally a son renounced his inheritance or the parents preferred to pass their *casa* on to a daughter. Daniel Castillo, Mariano Castillo, Domingo Bandrés, Juan Bandrés, Luis Solano, and Juan Solano were all eldest or only sons who were named heirs. But we have also seen that Angela Iglesias, Antonia Clavero and her mother, and Sebastiana Bandrés, none of whom had brothers, inherited their parents' *casas*. In 1971, when I surveyed the houses that had been passed on to their owners through inheritance, 60 percent were inherited by males, most of them oldest sons.

Inheritance was impartible, but all children had a claim to their parents' estate unless it was compensated for by the heir, or by the parents in the heir's name. Customarily parents paid, or enjoined their heir to pay, non-inheriting siblings a dowry (*una dote;* in Aragon often called *un arreglo*, a settlement) in exchange for their renouncing a share of the estate and their right to live at home. Male and female children were treated equally in this regard—they received the same settlement or its equivalent. Wealthier couples gave non-heirs money, a house, an education, or a piece of land, as well as household furnishings. Poorer ones gave furnishings and a token payment in money. Many very poor couples gave nothing and

3. See Merino y Hernández, *Aragón y su derecho.*

did not even name an heir—they could not afford to pay the notary to draw up the land-transfer papers.

Wealthy couples, those who had substantial property at stake and money available to pay a notary, drew up marriage contracts (*capitulaciones matrimoniales*) which specified the heir, the dowries paid to non-inheriting siblings, the rights of parents, and the obligations of the inheriting couple. When an heir married a non-heir, the marriage contract named the latter's financial contribution to the marriage, the dowry, and specified one or more of the heir's fields as its equivalent. The dowry could be reclaimed in the form of the field if the marriage was annulled or if the spouse who had contributed it became widowed and remarried. If he or she did not remarry, contracts usually specified the spouse's right to live in the heir's house and to govern half the fruits of the estate. Marriage contracts were always limited to wealthier families in Ibieca, but even among them contracts became less common after 1900. Such arrangements that irrevocably linked marriage and inheritance (called marriage-succession arrangements in the anthropological literature) made sense from the point of view of both parents and children as long as life expectancy was short and couples married late. Parents settled their estates late in their lives, and young couples were not subjected to parental rule for long. During this century, as lifespans increased and marriage ages declined,[4] marriage-succession arrangements bound parents and heir to an irrevocable arrangement for an increasing number of years. Some, perhaps preferring less binding arrangements, have decided not to draw up marriage contracts.

When there was no marriage contract, parents usually drew up a will, often long after the designated heir had married. From the parents' point of view, the advantage of a will was that they did not have to pay the fee to transfer the property; rather, their heir did, after their death. Also, in principle, they could maintain more control over the fate of the estate because they held the threat of disinheritance. Of course, the threat was tempered by the heir designate's right to abandon the parents and the estate, as Bernardo

---

4. I have figures on the age of marriage only since the Civil War, based on church records. The average age at marriage of twelve couples between 1939 and 1943 was twenty-seven for women and thirty-four for men. For fifteen couples between 1956 and 1968, it was twenty-six for women and thirty-one for men.

Loriente and his wife, Julia Janovas, did before the Civil War. Which threat held sway probably varied with economic options elsewhere. When they were good, the heir designate had an upper hand; when they were not, the parents did.

Whatever the formal arrangement, the customary understanding was that parents had the right to live in their house, to share its fruits, and to be cared for by the inheriting couple as they grew unable to care for themselves. Unmarried siblings who had not taken their dowries had similar rights. These inheritance customs generated stem families (that is, married couples living with one or more of their parents) over the course of family cycles. In 1950 one-third of Ibieca's households were centered on stem families.[5]

Within the family system, the lines of authority and power ran from parents to married heirs to unmarried siblings to children. As parents retired from working actively, the inheriting couple acquired more power in the household and became its social center. Around the inheriting couple other family members filled three kinds of roles: children, the retired head couple, and unmarried or widowed siblings of the active and retired heirs. The privileges, rights, and duties of young children and definitively retired elders were clear and unequivocal. Older men and women, especially when widowed, held a special station in village life, having fulfilled their worldly duties. In contrast, there was nothing privileged about children in old Ibieca. The children of most households were set to work full-time by the age of eight or ten, either at home or, often, in other households in exchange for room and board. Children were appreciated for the labor they contributed to a household, as well as for their potential economic and social return to it.

Clear but more problematic was the transition zone between the active and retiring couples. The issues of the transition and the terms of settlement were fairly explicit in the case of men, and who would make what decisions about how to plant and work what fields was clearly stated. So were the economic obligations of the inheriting couple to the parent couple. Obligations and rights that fell within the female domain were worked out "behind the scenes"

5. Based on village census records. Berkner, "The Stem Family," has shown that vagaries in the domestic cycles of families always suppress the actual incidence of stem families.

rather than explicitly; perhaps for that reason, the relationship between women in transit with respect to the position of head couple of a household was one of the tensest and most tribulating in that world of otherwise well-worn solutions.[6] In the early 1970s relations beween two mothers and their daughters-in-law were so strained that they had not been speaking to each other for years, even though they lived under the same roof.

Potential tension between the inheriting couple and resident siblings was defused, though not eliminated, by the simple fact that the siblings were unmarried. More than one married sibling never occupied the same household, and that married sibling was either the head, the former head, or the heir. The lower status of non-heir siblings was reinforced by their celibacy in Ibieca, because marriage was the principal definition of full adulthood. Single persons were not quite adults; in my experience in Ibieca, those over forty were neither as serious nor taken as seriously as married adults. They were unconstrained by the obligations that are acquired in making a family of one's own. They somehow spoke too freely, and they were spoken of freely by others, which in Ibieca constitutes a form of disrespect. None of them was forbidden to marry, none consciously chose celibacy, and each had tales told about missed marital chances. They found places at home because their labor and affection were needed, but they could stay only as long as they did not marry, which rendered them subordinate.

In contrast to these unequal aspects of family roles were a set of ideas and a code of conduct—an ethic and etiquette—about the good worker (*buen trabajador*) that all family members shared. A good man worked every possible hour of every day to maintain and build the family's patrimony; he planned ahead and was prepared for unpredictable events. He did not drink excessively; he was composed and respected in public places; he kept his word; he saved money rather than spent it. A good woman met similar standards for work and public interactions, though she was less visible and more restrained in public than men were expected to be. Women did not drink in public, their conversations were scorned as gossip, and there were considerable restrictions placed on their movements and

6. See Harding, "Women and Words," pp. 293–94.

their interactions with men, especially before marriage. Opposed to this ethic of proper character and behavior were images of the bad person, again defined in terms of an individual's effect on the family reputation and the *casa*'s viability. The big spender (*gastador*) squandered household wealth by gambling, making bad deals or investments, buying luxuries, or going into debt to provide big dowries. The vain or presumptuous person (*fanfarrón* or *presumador*) wasted money on fine clothes and other self-indulgences and was not a serious worker. When someone's bad behavior resulted in the downfall of a *casa* through the sale of its lands and livestock, he or she was called an *acabador*, a destroyer.

All the stories I was told about *casas* that declined during the last century focused on a person, as often a man as a woman, or a couple whose bad habits and ideas ravaged and dissolved the family estate. In the latter part of the nineteenth century Baltazar Abadías pawned his estate away providing dowries for his eight daughters. Andrés Castro's widowed stepmother drank too much, squandered money, and let the fields go to weed around 1905. Andrés revived the estate, but Casa Capablo and Casa Panzano were completely dismantled by spendthrift and indolent heirs. More recently, around 1950, Miguel Bierge's widow had to sell his house and lands to pay debts he had incurred by making bad investments in Huesca capital for many years.

For men and women, rich and poor, definitions of right and wrong and of good and bad character were grounded in the well-being, prosperity, and continuity of the *casa*. Codes of conduct and character, inculcated primarily by parents and the priest, regulated relations with near and distant kin, with neighbors and with strangers, and with potential spouses and in-laws. Marital decisions were pivotal for a *casa*'s survival. Clearly, the *casa*'s future hung in the balance with the marriage of the heir. A squandering, lazy, slandering spouse could ruin a *casa* in a matter of a few years. Morally, though not necessarily financially, as bad, a daughter might become pregnant, or a son might get a girl pregnant, and they and their parents would carry around the shame of a hasty private predawn wedding or an illegitimate child for the rest of their lives. Premarital pregnancies blackened a family's name, but they were rather common and not infrequently forced a marriage that the parents did not want. It was a subject not often discussed, but of the sixty married women in Ibieca in the early 1970s, I knew of a half-dozen who had been pregnant when they married, and there were no doubt others.

More often, especially among heirs, marriages were timely. Ideally the spouse was frugal, hardworking, and clever, someone who fortified a *casa* and could take advantage of changing circumstances. Sometimes a marriage between two families was so propitious that it was duplicated. After his first wife died, Andrés Castro married her sister. Shortly after Eugenio Clavero's marriage, his widowed father married his wife's widowed mother. Not long after a young man from Casa Sánchez married a young woman from Casa Abad, the young man's sister married the young woman's brother. When Luis Solano married Pilar Nueno, it was the second marriage between the two families; his father and her mother were siblings, both from Casa Solano. Juan Blanco's older brother also married his first cousin. The Castro-Bandrés and Sánchez-Abad marriages linked two well-to-do *casas* in Ibieca. Eugenio's and his father's marriages combined their poorer households. The Blanco and Solano marriages joined and rejoined those families from Ibieca with high mountain village families, giving the Solanos and the Blancos access to high mountain pastures for their sheep and to families who raised livestock and draft animals.

In old Ibieca most villagers cast out of their natal homes by the impartible inheritance system married into other houses, or set up their own, in Ibieca and surrounding villages. The economy and society of the area was sufficiently open and fluid so that newly married couples without dowries not infrequently rented, bought, or built a house in the village, and some acquired a patrimony over the years. Single siblings who moved out of the *casa* sometimes stayed in a Somontano village as full-time workers for other families. Most other siblings (married and single) moved to Huesca, Barcelona, Zaragoza, and sometimes Madrid. Around the turn of the century several dozen villagers went to Buenos Aires; most who went so far never returned, and some were never heard from again.

Over generations, marriages by the siblings of heirs into *casas* in Ibieca and other central Somontano villages produced a dense, seamless web of kin and affinal relations. The intermarriages were one source of the sense of belonging, of familiarity and communality, that was still palpable in the early 1970s. Each family was directly related to a number of other families in Ibieca, and each of them in turn was related to still others in the village, so that eventually, through relations of relations, almost everyone in Ibieca was vaguely related. Each family was also directly related to families in other villages which repeated the same pattern in Ibieca, so that eventually, through relations of relations, almost everyone in the Somontano was diffusely related. An individual's effective kinship network, however, spanned three generations and included lateral as well as lineal relations: parents, their siblings and children; one's spouse and his or her parents, siblings, and their families; one's own siblings and their immediate families; one's children and their families.

The fate, marital and otherwise, of siblings was less crucial to the welfare and continuity of a *casa* than was the heir's fate, but it was still important, especially if they remained in the Somontano. Whether single or married, siblings might be called upon for labor or loans in time of need. Their marriages transformed more kith into kin who might be called on for a variety of favors and exchanges. They also provided contacts for jobs and places to stay for the heir's children during fiestas, which were ends in themselves and also the major means of meeting potential spouses. Finally, if an inheriting couple was childless, they might turn to their nieces and nephews in search of an heir. Sara Segarra's father, Fernando, was a nephew named heir and thus catapulted from *la parte baja* to *la parte alta* in Ibieca. He became known as a generous *amo* to his workers and was not as active in caciqual politics as were Solano, Blanco, and Costa. Nevertheless, he was allied with his wealthy and influential neighbors and was persecuted as a fascist during the war. His story, like Andrés Castro's, pits a good man against a squandering woman in a struggle to maintain the *casa*, and it describes the fate of three generations of Segarra siblings.

Fernando inherited Casa Segarra, an estate of some fifty hectares, from his uncle José. José married around 1870. His wife bore seven children, all of whom died in infancy, and she died bearing the seventh. José remarried; his second wife, Faustina, bore no children.

José's three sisters married and moved to surrounding Somon-tano villages. His brother, Vicente, married Domingo Bandrés's sis-ter, Teresa. Vicente received no dowry, but Teresa's father bought them a house for her dowry, and Vicente set up a small store and butcher shop in the patio. Though it was illegal, Vicente also made liquor from anise in the stable next to the patio and traveled around the Somontano selling it. Vicente had to give this up when he was caught by customs guards on a village raid. They arrived just as he was carrying the still out of the house to hide it from them, and he was fined a hundred pesetas.

Vicente and Teresa had three daughters and a son, Fernando. One daughter married the heir of a small landholding casa in Ibieca; another married a worker and moved to Madrid; the third never married and worked as a domestic servant for a family in Zaragoza for fifty years.

José Segarra had named Fernando heir of his estate, but he changed his will when Fernando married Gregoria Lobera and sailed to Buenos Aires in 1913 with no intention of returning. At first José willed the estate to his wife; then, shortly before he died in 1920, he rewrote his will again, naming Fernando or Fernando's eldest son the principal heir and dividing about one-third of the estate up among his other nieces and nephews. Although they were doing well in Buenos Aires and had bought a house and some land, Fernando decided to return to Ibieca after José died.

In the meantime the estate, already reduced by the terms of Jo-sé's will, was further reduced by his widow. The will entitled her to the income from half the estate's harvests as long as she lived and gave her the right to dispose of the casa's movable property. Before Fernando returned, Faustina sold almost everything that moved or could be moved. She sent servants to surrounding villages to sell sheets, kitchenware, and other household goods, and she sold their draft animals, sheep, chickens, hens, and rabbits to her neighbors. Faustina put the money she earned from the sales and from her half of the dwindling harvests in a joint account with her brother in Huesca. Fernando and Gregoria restocked the house when they re-turned with the small fortune they had accumulated in Buenos Aires. They also bought back most of the fields that Fernando's uncle had willed to his cousins and siblings, and they recovered

Fernando Segarra's family, around 1945

the estate's former stature. Faustina continued to put her half of its
income into the bank account with her brother, who inherited it
when she died.

Fernando and Gregoria had six children, four daughters and two
sons. They sent their eldest son to earn a degree as a village secre-
tary, and he obtained a post in a high mountain village. Their el-
dest daughter married the tenant of a large estate outside Huesca.
Another daughter became a domestic servant for a Zaragoza fam-
ily, whom she met through her aunt, and never married. Sara
Segarra married Mariano Castillo, and her younger sister, Angela,
married Tomás Lacasa. Both men were from families that had been
pitted against the Segarras during the Civil War, but they had es-
tablished themselves in commerce since the war, and Sara and
Angela overrode their father's objections in making the ties. Luis,
the second son, was named heir of Casa Segarra when he married
Lucia Abadía, a woman from a poor casa around the corner, also
among the reds during the Civil War.

The Segarra family, though well off, was not above sending a
daughter into domestic service with another family; the Blanco and
Solano families were. Both Juan Blanco and Luis Solano had sisters
who never married and lived at home all their lives, helping their
sisters-in-law manage the *casas.* Marriages in these two families
were likewise more status conscious, more strategic. Luis, his father, and his aunt intermarried with wealthy mountain families, as
did Juan and his older brother, who studied medicine and set up
practice in Benasque, at the foot of the highest peak in the Pyrenees.
Juan's father married another of Luis's aunts, so Juan and Luis were
first cousins. Two of Luis's siblings "married the church" (one became a nun, the other a priest) and his other two brothers married
heirs to wealthy *casas* in nearby villages. Of Juan's three other siblings, only one, the third and youngest son, married beneath his
station. His wife was the heir of yet another small landholding *casa*
in Ibieca that had allied with the reds during the war and turned to
commerce afterward. One sister married an heir to a wealthy Velillas *casa,* and the other married an officer in the Bank of Spain in
Madrid.

Marriages in old Ibieca were not dictated by parents, though parents sometimes succeeded in vetoing a child's choice or in arranging a match to which the child consented. Wealthy parents in particular sometimes urged marriages that protected or augmented their political or productive power, but even modest landholders at least tried to insure that their heirs made good marriages. Parents with modest landholdings whose heir-designate did not locate a spouse on his or her own might consult one or two women in Ibieca who specialized in knowing about available young men and women and their endowments. One of the last, if not the last, arranged marriages in Ibieca was between Antonia Encontra and Clemente Azlor shortly after the war. Antonia was nearly thirty, the heir of a fairly substantial *casa* of twenty hectares, and she had no groom in sight. Clemente was the foreman for a wealthy *casa* in Arbaniés when he heard of Antonia's availability through one of the local matchmakers. He paid a formal call on Antonia's parents, then visited Antonia a few times, and they decided to marry.

The children of wealthy *casas* could afford the time and expense involved in visiting relatives in other villages on their own and so set up their own marriage circuit. Other villagers were limited to family rites (weddings and funerals), fiestas, and wage work as means of meeting potential spouses beyond the village boundaries. Fiestas (especially for heirs) and wage work (for non-heirs) were by far the most common occasions on which intervillage matches were made.

Fiestas were, among other things, extended rituals in which families from various *casas* related by blood and marriage renewed and celebrated their connections. Several days each year were designated as national or international fiestas by the Catholic Church, and each village had its own long-standing major and minor fiesta days in the names of patron saints. Ibieca's major fiesta was on Saint Clemente's Day, November 23; its minor fiesta was on the Day of the Virgin, September 8. In addition, each family had a fiesta on the day of the saint after whom the male head of the household was named. The main family event on all the fiestas was a midday meal to which the families of siblings of the active heads of the household were invited. During village fiestas there were also special masses, prayers, and processions in the name of the patron saint.

There were two sites where potential spouses might meet. One

Iglesias kin at a fiesta-day meal

was at the dinner table, since cousins often invited a friend or neighbor to join their family's fiesta meal. The other was on the village dance floor. During village fiestas two or three nights of dancing lasted until early morning. Under the eyes of kin, friends, and neighbors, young men and women from many villages noticed each other, were introduced, talked, and danced. Such dances were still held in the 1970s, and the air was always charged with watchfulness on the part of both elders and youth. As young men and women paired off and danced, they gambled the fates of their *casas*. Bad matches were as common as good ones, and either might have effects beyond the families involved, so everyone, even neighbors and friends, monitored the matches as they danced by.

Lines of Power and Solidarity

Most of the social and economic connections discussed above were also political connections. Some set up power differentials between individuals in different social roles and categories; others equalized power among individuals, minimized social distinctions, and facilitated communal action.

Two broad political principles, one egalitarian and the other hierarchical, crisscrossed Ibieca's *casas*, the village itself, and the Somontano in general. Most activities and social relations contained elements of both principles. The inheritance system emphasized the hierarchy between parents and children,[7] while the ethic of the good worker stressed action by all family members for the common good of the family. Marriage, neighborliness, and resource sharing were all fairly egalitarian and mutualistic relations between families; relations among agricultural workers, among domestic workers, and among *amos*, while often competitive, were also in some ways egalitarian. Of course, hierarchy was stressed in relations between *amos* and their servants and workers, but even so, there was a kind of intimacy between some *amo* and laboring families that contradicted the inequality.[8]

The *amos'* domination of other village families was formalized in their control of municipal government—except during the Republic and the Civil War—and it was paralleled by Catholic rituals and the relationship of the priest to villagers.[9] Angela Iglesias described prewar *amos* and priests in similar terms: they were greater than ordinary persons, almost like lords. To some extent, the larger hierarchies from which bosses and priests derived their powers were gender specific. Village men were more engaged by and with the political hierarchy, and women with the religious one. Saints, Mary, and God were more real to Angela Iglesias, Sara Segarra, and many other village women than were ministers, governors, and heads of state. Here again, distinctions also created similarities and solidarity of men, of women, and of villagers as commoners in relation to their sacred and secular rulers.

The crisscrossing of hierarchical and egalitarian principles united the village into a whole rife with contradictions. Depending on the issues, the context, and the subtle play of history and personalities, the whole might act in concert or shatter into factions. The following story from prewar Ibieca illustrates a rare moment in which the village united to defend a common good.

7. Cole and Wolf, *Hidden Frontier*, discuss the family ideologies organized by partible and impartible inheritance systems in the Italian Alps.

8. Barrett, "Social Hierarchy and Intimacy," discusses social intimacy between high- and low-ranking houses in Benabarre, east of Ibieca.

9. Christian, *Person and God*, discusses both hierarchies and their parallelism in a Cantabrian valley.

Water was both an unwieldy and an invaluable resource and hence a frequent source of conflict, as was the case in a dispute between Angüés and Ibieca in 1922. Although the problem was actually perpetrated by one household in Angüés, the villagers of Ibieca spoke as if Angüés as a whole were responsible. A wealthy and ambitious landowner from Angüés, Enrique Calasanz, bought a garden in Ibieca on the downward slope from the fountain. The garden's spring and the village fountain were fed by the same underground stream. It became apparent that Calasanz's plan was to build a pipe from the spring to his own land in Angüés, about six miles to the south. Villagers were convinced that, if Calasanz drew off water for his lands from the spring, their own fountain, and thus their gardens, would dry up. Their collective existence threatened, villagers united and prepared to defend their water with arms.

When a sentry spotted the carriage bringing Calasanz and an engineer to survey the garden plot and the path of the pipe, he rang the church bells to call village men from the fields. By the time the men arrived, all able-bodied women in the village were standing by the fountain, armed with pitchforks and scythes. The men took up their own weapons and reinforced their wives and mothers. If Calasanz and the engineer had approached them, there would have been a confrontation. Violence was averted only because they first called on Casa Solano, perhaps as a courtesy and without any awareness of the opposition that awaited them. Luis Solano informed them that they would be wise to abandon their plans. They did so for the day, and eventually they abandoned the project completely. Calasanz tried to secure support from authorities in Huesca, but he failed because Luis Solano had already contacted them and convinced them to support Ibieca's claim to water over Calasanz's right to pipe it to Angüés.

Part Two
The Formation of
Farmers, 1950-75

❧ Chapter Four
❧ Market, State,
❧ and Countryside
❧ under Franco

The sense of connectedness, the complex social and political webs among families, and the labyrinth of rules generating them are dissolving in contemporary Ibieca. Through a protracted series of discrete individual decisions to alter the conduct of agriculture in response to state reforms and changing markets, villagers have, in effect, dismantled the peasant and early capitalist productive forms that organized social life in the Somontano for over a century. By 1975, the social relations of agricultural production were dominated by the requirements of capital, not labor; of the market, not the *casa*. The two forms of production had collapsed into one advanced capitalist form with several variations. The villagers remade Ibieca, and they remade themselves in the process. In 1950, Ibieca was a village of peasants, *amos*, and agricultural laborers; by 1975, it was a village of farmers and wage workers.

This chapter traces the state policies and programs and changing market conditions that altered the context of village agriculture, placing them in the historical context of the postwar black market years and in the international context of U.S. intervention in the Spanish economy, both direct and via the Spanish state.[1]

Black Market Years

The Civil War devastated the Spanish agricultural economy. In 1940 crop and livestock production was at 80 percent of its pre-

---

1. My principal sources on state policies and programs under Franco were: Tamames, *Estructura económica* and *República*; López de Sebastián, *Política agraria*; Herr, *Spain*; Aceves, *Changing Faces*; Marti, "Agriculture in Politics"; agricultural officials in Huesca, mainly in COSA and the Ministry of Agriculture; and villagers.

war level.[2] Tens of thousands of work animals had been slaughtered to feed troops, many agricultural machines were beyond repair, and Spain was subject to a nearly universal trade embargo established by western nations. The primary agrarian goal of General Francisco Franco's regime during the 1940s was to restore private production, both peasant and early capitalist, sufficiently to feed people in both cities and countryside.

Among the first agrarian agencies of the Franco state was the National Service of Socioeconomic Land Reform (SNREST), set up in 1938 behind Nationalist lines with a mandate to restore to their prewar owners estates expropriated by collectives during the war. In effect, the agency managed the large landowners' recovery of property and economic power. The task accomplished in 1939, SNREST was converted into the National Institute of Colonialization (INC). Modeled on an agency set up in Italy under Mussolini, during the 1940s INC conducted several large-scale irrigation projects in zones dominated by big estates. Estate owners either enjoyed irrigation rights for a modest fee, or they were bought out at exorbitant prices and their estates were divided into small properties and sold to landless families at modest prices. INC also built villages for these "colonists."

In addition, the 1940s saw a token effort at establishing a minimum wage in the countryside and a much more elaborate series of efforts to control agricultural and food prices. Agricultural wage levels were set nationally, and they were theoretically administered in three zones. But according to an agrarian official in Huesca, most villagers did not even know what the minimum wages were, and the wages paid were consistently below the minimum. Prices for many goods were set, and essential foodstuffs were rationed. All families were issued ration books for bread, olive oil, rice, chickpeas, beans, and a few other essentials. With them they bought fixed amounts of each item every month at official prices. Commerce in these foodstuffs was likewise state regulated. The General Commission of Supplies and Transportation (CGAT) was their legal buyer, except in the case of wheat, and CGAT agents regulated storage, transport, processing, and sale of these items.

During the Civil War Franco's government established the Na-

2. Marti, "Agriculture and Politics," p. 154.

tional Wheat Service (SNT), which expropriated the wheat market from private hands. Through the SNT the state became the exclusive legal buyer of wheat from producers, the exclusive seller to flour mills, and it regulated the sale of flour to bakeries. The state set prices at each point for wheat, flour, and bread. In the case of feed cereals, the state bought them at a fixed price but did not outlaw the private market.

Where the state outlawed the private market there flourished a black market. Julian Pitt-Rivers estimated that half of all food produced in Alcalá, an Andalusian village, was sold on the black market. Government officials estimated that substantially more wheat was sold on the black market than to the SNT in the early postwar years, and Henri Marti calculated that cereal incomes increased over 50 percent during the 1940s due to black market sales.[3] Gerald Brenan, also writing of Andalusia, said that people of all social classes were involved in the black market. Those with land marketed their crops illegally; those who could afford to pay twice the official prices bought black market goods; those who could not afford the prices registered false births and concealed deaths to maximize their rations.[4] The state inspectors (*fiscales*) were the terror of village life those years—they had the right to inspect premises and confiscate any rationed goods in excess of monthly quotas. Their course was steered by denouncements, which they rewarded with a portion of the goods confiscated, and by bribes—their cut of goods not confiscated.[5]

In Ibieca, as in many Spanish villages, the women of poorer households continuously trafficked in modest quantities of small goods, transporting eggs, chickens, and vegetables past inspection officers posted on the outskirts of Huesca by slipping the items into baskets or hiding them under their skirts, later to sell them to friends and small merchants in the city.[6] Black market olives and olive oil were usually trafficked by the man licensed in each village to transport those products for official sale. He was issued a permit for each trip from the village to the olive mill with olives, and back

3. Pitt-Rivers, *People of the Sierra*, p. 20; Marti, "Agriculture and Politics," p. 192.
4. Brenan, *Face of Spain*, pp. 105, 115.
5. Ibid., p. 216.
6. See Fraser, *In Hiding*.

again with oil; instead of running one trip with each permit, he ran two. The miller, for his part, worked his mill sixteen hours a day instead of the eight he was permitted by CGAT. Finally, each village household carted its own black market wheat directly to a local flour miller under the cover of darkness, rather than taking it to the SNT in Huesca.

Villages were assigned quotas of wheat to produce for SNT. In theory, these quotas represented the maximum amount agriculturists could be expected to produce, minus whatever they needed for seed and household consumption. Later, quotas were set lower than the theoretical surplus produced—how much lower depended on friendships between influential villagers and the SNT officials in Huesca who set the quotas.[7] Given its quota, the village government was responsible for distributing it among village households, thus providing influential villagers with another opportunity to advance their own interests. At first Roberto Barrio, a small landowner, worked on the committee that distributed the quota in Ibieca. The committee, controlled by large landowners, placed the burden of meeting the quota on small landowners, and Roberto decided to quit rather than cooperate with the favoritism. As before the war, *amos* were able to turn governmental policies to their own benefit—they were still *caciques*.

Black market prices were double the official prices and, while most villagers engaged in black market selling, the profits were spread unevenly. On the provincial level, the big estate owners, millers, bakers, and major olive oil transporters earned large fortunes. In Ibieca, large landowners made small fortunes on their wheat and olive oil surpluses, but many small owners also made unprecedented profits during the 1940s. Overall, black market production, supplemented by the stabilizing effects of the SNT, resulted in the recovery of both peasants and *amos* in Ibieca by 1950.

Franco's ultimate concern during the 1940s was maintaining and consolidating his control of state power. Franco had allied with large landowners during the Civil War and, like Primo de Rivera before him, he avoided attacking them directly. Indeed, they fattened themselves considerably on SNT wheat policies and other govern-

7. See Marti, "Agriculture and Politics," ch. 5.

ment programs. In some ways, however, Franco's regime compromised caciqual political power from the beginning. Appointments of mayors and civil governors were tightly controlled from the center. The national parliament was reestablished, but most of its members were ex officio or appointed, and the rest were selected through centrally controlled elections. All political organizing outside the Falange (the official party) was prohibited. Furthermore, nationalization of the wheat market and controls on the marketing of other cereals robbed provincial *caciques* of a major source of their power.

United States Intervention

Toward the end of the 1940s, due to mounting pressure from slowly reorganizing opposition groups in the context of a vast black market and an underdeveloped economy, Franco's government entered a crisis of political survival. A secret telegram sent by the American chargé in Spain, Paul T. Culbertson, to the secretary of state on February 17, 1949, recounted the gravity of Franco's situation and pinpointed American policy considerations that proved decisive for Spain's future:

> Information we obtain lends definite color prediction possible economic collapse in Spain in six months or so in absence outside aid. Embassy not prepared concur fully . . . since Spain over centuries shown ability live on little or nothing. However, if present drought continues, causing poor crops and increasingly severe electricity restrictions, if private enterprises continue unable meet bank obligations, if Argentina does not supply wheat or should curtail present credits and Spain's grain crop should be failure, I do not see how Spain's economic and social structure can hold together indefinitely. . . .
> As seriousness situation increases pressure of necessity might well bring about change present economic policies and shake up government. Mild rumors latter point persist. However Franco could be stubborn enough pull temple down on selves especially since unable determine what concrete bene-

fits, if any, might come from outside were he adopt new policies, new measures. Economic breakdown by no means certainty, but clearly possibility. It would seriously affect Spanish political stability with no immediate alternative to replace Franco which could control situation.

Economic and political breakdown or disintegration in Spain bound have severe repercussions on our aims economic political rehabilitation Europe. Such eventuality not in our interest nor that France and UK. I feel risk should be weighed carefully against present political objections. If they not overriding suggest as first step (if we wish avoid risk breakdown) offer Spain immediate access equal terms with others [at Export-Import] Bank, leaving to bank determination credit risk and conditions. In exchange obtain from Spanish government assurances fair equal treatment American trade and investment.[8]

Franco did not prove so stubborn. His dire political straits converged with the need of the United States to make Spain a node in the vast international military and economic network it was constructing in its conduct of the Cold War. U.S. military men argued that Spain's location at the neck of the Mediterranean made its active allegiance vital to Europe's "collective security" against the Soviet Union, and Franco's anti-communism became more important than his fascism.

In the late 1940s, as an adjunct to the Marshall Plan to finance the capitalist reconstruction of northwestern Europe, the United States lifted the boycott of Spain which had been imposed in protest of Franco's dictatorship and accorded his regime formal recognition. The day after Chargé Culbertson sent his telegram, the Chase Manhattan Bank indicated "that Spanish officials were now willing to remedy objectionable economic practices and policies in order to qualify for further private or official U.S. loans."[9] Chase had just completed negotiations on the first U.S. loan to Spain since the Civil War; that $25 million opened the way for further foreign loans. In 1950 Congress voted to loan $62.5 million to Spain, and in 1953 a

8. United States, Department of State, *Foreign Relations*, pp. 729–30. I am grateful to Marilyn Young for this reference.

9. Ibid., p. 729 n. 3.

treaty was signed giving Spain extensive military and economic aid in exchange for the right to build U.S. military bases on Spanish soil. In 1959 as a stipulation for further aid, Spanish economic policies were revamped and domestic markets were opened to multinational penetration. By 1965 the United States had given Franco's government about $1.8 billion in aid. In the words of Richard Herr: "With the United States behind him, Franco became virtually unassailable at home and abroad."[10]

Recent capitalist development in Spain, in agriculture as well as industry and finance, must be viewed in the context of Spain's alliance with the United States. According to Herr, "As to other sectors of the economy, the military agreement with the United States gave an impetus to agricultural reform. The two countries exchanged agricultural experts, and gave grants and loans to the Spanish agencies furthering agricultural improvement. By 1963 Spain had received $90 million for this purpose. The sum is not large, but it offered the marginal outlay the country needed."[11] The loans and aid not only provided the funds for reconstruction and development; they also defined their content and determined their direction. The policies, programs, agencies, incentives, and organizations of the Spanish state under Franco reshaped agricultural production and rural life, including Ibieca's. And those policies, in turn, were shaped by the terms and stipulations contained in loans, grants, and aid coming, above all, from the United States government and private banks.

The Agrarian Reform Programs

The Spanish government, through the uncoordinated offices of a dozen major ministries, commissions, and boards, reorganized the conduct of agriculture during the 1950s and 1960s in the direction of capital intensification and commercialization. Both peasant and early capitalist agriculturalist were thrown into crises. Those who responded by pursuing the incentives for change inadvertently dissolved the customary forms of production and more thoroughly incorporated Ibieca and other villages into larger national and inter-

10. Herr, *Spain*, p. 239.
11. Ibid., p. 247.

national economic structures as these evolved an advanced capitalist form of agricultural production.

Two sorts of measures were taken by state agencies in the reorganization of agriculture. The first were *direct reform* efforts which explicitly targeted a village or area for development. The biggest schemes were the irrigation and colonization projects organized by INC. During the 1950s and 1960s so many dams were built and there was so much hoopla about each one that Franco was nicknamed *el sapo* (the toad), as if he were leaping from reservoir to reservoir. In 1952 the National Service of Plot Consolidation (SNCP) was organized. When half of the landowners in a village petitioned for it, SNCP agents surveyed and organized the redistribution of all village land so that each landowner's patrimony was concentrated into one continuous estate, instead of broken into many small and scattered plots. This change enabled owners to work their land more efficiently. Various agencies, including the SNCP, facilitated the organization of production and distribution cooperatives. Under a comprehensive program, Rural Regulation (Ordenación Rural), whole areas were designated for special development and controls—plot consolidation, irrigation, production and distribution cooperatives, and other reforms. Again, the area's designation depended on a majority of families consenting to it. In 1973 these overt reform activities carried out by INC and SNCP came under the control of one agency—the Institute of Agrarian Reform and Development (IRYDA).

The above-named agencies and programs directly intervened and developed capitalist agriculture in some parts of Spain, but not in the Somontano. The only scheme that would have directly affected the Somontano's agriculture was the Calcon dam project. The plan was to build a dam north of Ibieca in the Sierra de Guara and irrigate some fields in villages to the south from its reservoir. The dam was first proposed by the Spanish government in 1910 but never got beyond the planning stage. The project was reactivated under Franco in the 1950s, some work was completed, and then it was once again abandoned. This is as close as the central Somontano came to being part of an explicit plan to develop agricultural production under Franco.

Ibieca's economy was reorganized by the second broad category of reforms, *indirect reforms*, that affected the conditions of agricultural production. Of the indirect reforms affecting Ibieca, those managed by the SNT and the Official Council of Agrarian Unions (COSA) had by far the greatest effects.

The state's policies and programs on wheat and other cereals and on the mechanization of cereal production went through three phases after 1949. The period from 1949 to 1958 was one of straightforward stimulation of wheat production. The goal was to produce enough wheat to meet domestic demand and halt foreign imports. The main mechanism was raising the price, which motivated producers to put more land in wheat. The hikes were substantial in absolute terms. The 1948 price was 1.6 pesetas per kilogram, in 1950 it was 3.4 pesetas. The SNT assumed real control of the wheat market after 1952, when rationing was abandoned and the black market dried up. By 1958 the price was 5.1 pesetas. For the period overall, in relative terms, the price of wheat rose faster than the cost of living.

Another major mechanism of promoting cereal cultivation was state involvement in tractor rentals and sales. There were very limited tractor sales in Huesca during the 1940s and 1950s, all of them regulated by the provincial Ministry of Agriculture. Landowners who wanted to buy tractors applied to the ministry. They had to meet qualifications, such as actively cultivating a certain number of hectares, but because there were more qualified applicants than tractors the ministry officials tended to award tractors to their rural friends and friends of friends. The result was that the most influential large landowners—the *caciques*—received the tractors. Some resold them for fantastic profits to other less influential landowners. In 1955 Juan and Luis Solano bought a new tractor at half price through the ministry. In 1956 Tomás Coronas, Gabriel Abadía, and Ricardo Sánchez bought used tractors at prices well above their legal market value from large landowners in other villages who had previously purchased them at discount prices through the ministry.

While some large landowners bought Ministry of Agriculture tractors during the mid-1950s, others, and many more modest landowners, rented them from the Official Council of Agrarian Unions (COSA). The COSA tractor rental program had an effect greatly out of proportion to its scale. Around 1952 ten to twenty tractors were sent to the provincial COSAs in wheat-producing areas of Spain. Twelve were sent to Huesca and, until 1963, COSA agents rented them by the hour to Somontano families to plow their land. The large but less influential landowners took most advantage of this program—Segarra, Coronas, Sánchez, Barraca. COSA rates were just high enough to pay the tractor driver and maintain the tractors. Through this program many medium and large landowners saw their land plowed faster and cheaper than work animals and men could plow them, and their yields increased markedly as a result of deeper plowing.

The second period of Spanish cereals policy lasted from 1958 to 1967. In 1958 domestic production of wheat met the demand for the first time, and state wheat policy went through a period of reformulation, as did Spanish economic policy in general. Price increases were continued during this period, though they did not match the rise in the cost of living, and the state elaborated and intensified its efforts to increase the productivity of wheat cultivation. In 1959 Spanish markets were opened to multinationals; indeed, the state facilitated corporate entry and expansion. Within a few years agricultural machinery, fertilizer, and high-yield seed grain, mainly from U.S.-controlled corporations, were available on a large scale for the first time in Spanish history.

Multinationals soon became a transforming force in Spanish agriculture in their own right, though independent family farmers continued to conduct production process. Subsidiaries of John Deere, Massey Ferguson, and Chrysler became the dominant suppliers of tractors and combines in the province during the 1960s, and three or four fertilizer companies affiliated with multinational chemical companies that over the fertilizer market. Multinationals affected the organization and content of crop production more or less indirectly, via the market conditions within which agricultural decisions were made. In the case of livestock production, multinational penetration was much more direct. During the 1960s vertically integrated livestock factories (*granjas integradas*) spread throughout the Somontano, and a half-dozen were set up by families in Ibieca. The *granjas*, raising chickens, hens, or pigs, were franchised by companies that were either owned or otherwise dominated by multinational feed companies such as Purina. By 1975 *granjas* produced

90 percent of the country's chicken and pork, and livestock production was as industrialized as agricultural production, an industrialization mediated more by multinational penetration than by agrarian reforms.[12]

The SNT made easy credit available for purchase of higher-yielding varieties of wheat seed and for chemical fertilizers. Mariano Castillo said that these products were, in fact, virtually given to producers for a period during the late 1950s. Also, for the first time in Spanish history, credit for major agricultural investments was made available on a substantial scale, and the terms for machinery loans were extraordinarily favorable. Banks were required by law to increase markedly the amount of agrarian credit available at low interest rates. In 1965 an agriculturalist could obtain a five-year loan to buy a tractor or combine from the state Bank of Agricultural Credit (BCA) through the Provincial Savings Bank of Huesca (Caja Rural) at 3 percent. In the late 1950s, Mariano recalled, the interest rate on machine loans was as low as 2.5 percent; moreover, the state at first subsidized purchases through outright grants. Using other subsidies as a standard, the state covered about 20 percent of many early machine purchases.

The Official Council of Agrarian Unions (COSA) also funneled funds through its village-level organizations, the Brotherhood of Agriculturalists and Livestock Owners (Hermandades), which petitioned loans from the provincial office of COSA. In 1967 Ibieca's Brotherhood, which all landowners were legally obliged to belong to, established its creditworthiness and borrowed 500,000 pesetas at 2.75 percent interest. The money was petitioned for general agricultural improvements and distributed to villagers in proportion to their landholdings. In 1968 Ibieca's Brotherhood borrowed another 500,000 pesetas, and in 1972 it borrowed 1,000,000 pesetas at 5 percent interest, expressly to improve the almond orchards owned by its members.

In 1963 the Ministry of Agriculture created associations to encourage the collective mechanization of small-scale wheat producers (ATCs). To qualify, each member of a proposed association had to

---

12. This discussion is based on an interview with Fernando Biarge, an executive of one of the Salas' corporations.

have fewer than 14 hectares, and the total amount of land held by group members had to be at least 50 hectares. Group members received credits for seed and fertilizer at 4 percent interest and subsidies of up to 1,200 pesetas per hectare for the first year of their association, as well as low-interest credit to buy machines and tools. The associations were required to carry on collectively for at least eight years; after that many dismantled because of accumulated friction over whose fields were to be plowed or harvested first.

Finally, through its *cupo* program in the 1960s, the state virtually gave all the diesel fuel that tractor and combine owners needed to work their crops. The program was intended to give machine owners coupons to cover half the cost of their fuel needs, but flagrant and widespread trickery permitted them to get all they needed for nothing.

The terms of agricultural credit continued to be easy during this period. Two figures give an idea of the expansion of credit: loans from the state Bank of Agricultural Credit in all of Spain rose from 400 million pesetas in 1952 to 4.5 billion pesetas in 1963.[13] In Huesca the BCA loaned, through the Official Council of the Agrarian Unions (COSA), 26 million pesetas to 1,168 borrowers in 1962; in 1965 it loaned 55 million pesetas to 2,297 borrowers.[14] A few figures on fertilizers and agricultural machines further indicate the effect of state activity: in 1952, 2.2 million kilograms of chemical fertilizers were spread in Huesca, and in 1968 78 million kilograms were used.[15] In 1958 there were 1,048 gas-oil tractors and 14 combines in the province; in 1967 there were 6,260 tractors and 1,078 combines.[16] In 1958 there were 4 tractors in Ibieca, and in 1967 there were 7 tractors and a combine.

The third period of Spanish wheat policies began in 1967. Moves were made by state agencies to support feed-cereal cultivation from the mid-1960s on, but with the huge wheat surpluses of 1967-68 the whole focus of state policy and programs shifted from wheat to feed cereals, setting a long-term goal of eliminating marginal producers

13. Herr, *Spain*, p. 249.
14. Consejo Económico Sindical Provincial de Huesca, *Ponencias*, p. 91.
15. Instituto Nacional de Estadística, *Reseña estadística* (1955).
16. I am grateful to the head of the Ministerio de Agricultura of Huesca for this information.

of both. The wheat price was frozen after 1967, and state prices for barley and oats were increased. The latter were higher than private market prices, high enough so that in many areas it was more profitable to sow feed cereals than wheat. Subsidies and easy credit for fertilizer and new varieties of seed were eliminated for wheat and established for feed cereals. The Ministry of Agriculture abolished the ATC arrangement for small and medium wheat producers and created a similar arrangement to subsidize larger landholders growing feed cereals. In 1969 Segarra, Barraca, Coronas, Abadía, and the Rivera brothers—four large landowners and the tenant of a large estate—availed themselves of this arrangement and bought a combine. To brake further mechanization by marginal producers of both wheat and cereals, the interest rate on ordinary machine loans was increased. By 1972 the Bank of Agricultural Credit's interest rate on farm machine loans was 5.5 percent, and in 1974 it was 6.5 percent—still modest, but significantly stiffer than the mid-1960s rate of 3 percent. The pace at which villagers bought tractors, however, did not abate; in 1975 there were twelve tractors and five combines in Ibieca.

In 1967 the SNT (National Wheat Service) was replaced by the SNC (National Cereals Service) and in 1970 the SNC was replaced by the SNPA (National Service of Agrarian Products). These organizational changes marked the end of wheat's central role in state agrarian subsidy programs and price policies. Those programs and policies were broadened to include, first, other cereals, then agrarian products in general. In 1973 the SNPA relinquished the state's monopoly over the wheat market, opening it to private millers and middlemen, and established a quota, based on past production, on how much wheat SNPA would buy from each producer. Thus the state was committed to wheat production up to a point; then it left producers to compete in a free market, which exposed them to pressure to be efficient or fold. According to Mariano Castillo, there were a number of ways in which wheat producers could weasel around their quota and sell their surplus to the state. Nevertheless, the message was clear to him and others: the state was moving against wheat, and the days of marginal cereal growers were numbered.

The state programs and incentives aimed at the mechanization and manipulation of cereal production included guaranteed purchase of cereals at good prices, tractor sale and rental programs, easy credit for purchasing tractors and combines, fertilizer and new varieties of cereal seed, substantial subsidies in the form of outright grants for purchasing machines, fertilizer, and seed, and the *cupo* program for fuel. These reforms were amplified by other programs affecting the fiscal, social, and physical infrastructure of the area, most of them carried out in the 1960s and early 1970s. The terms for land and home improvement loans were eased after the mid-1960s, and the overall level of loans to the Huesca countryside continued to increase rapidly. In 1966 the Provincial Rural Savings Bank loaned 38 million pesetas; in 1975 it loaned 2.3 billion pesetas.[17] In the late 1960s and early 1970s some of the following kinds of credit were available. First, there were low-interest loans for farm buildings with state subsidies of up to 20 percent. In 1973, for example, Tomás Coronas uprooted two dozen ancient olive trees to build a huge machinery shed with an agricultural loan and a 20 percent state subsidy. Second, colonization credit, or credit to clear land, was available at 2.75 percent with twenty to twenty-five years to pay. Third, one could obtain easy credit to buy cars and trucks. Fourth, credit to renovate houses could be had at 3 percent, repayable over a fifteen-year period after a five-year grace period, from the Provincial Rural Savings Bank of Huesca. If the loan was for under 10,000 pesetas, no interest was charged. No-interest loans of up to 25,000 pesetas were available from the Falange for household improvements. Whatever the source of the loan, the state would throw in 10,000 pesetas as a subsidy. Many villagers were cashing in on these terms and subsidies when I was in Ibieca.

In addition, during the 1960s and early 1970s the state under Franco paid for or subsidized a vastly improved provincial road system which was crucial to commercial agriculture and to making the countryside into a market for urban-produced goods. Two other pieces of state-financed infrastructure crucial to commercial agriculture were a network of modern silos, which cut the transportation costs of cereal growers, and a network of agricultural extension agencies, which gave classes and individual lectures as well as tai-

17. Caja Rural Provincial de Huesca, *Memoria.*

lor-made advice to agriculturalists. A silo was built in Angüés while I was in Ibieca, and an agricultural extension agent has been stationed there since 1972.

The state paid for substantial improvements in rural schooling, though rural education is still considerably below urban standards. In many villages the state split the cost of installing running water and sewage systems. And in the 1960s the state established a social security system and health insurance plans to cover most major medical expenses.

Some of the money destined for these social services was siphoned off or diverted to special interests. In 1948 there was a great scandal in Ibieca when it was discovered that the village secretary and the construction boss had embezzled substantial sums of money previously allotted to build the modern village schoolhouse. At the provincial level, where the architectural plans for new schools were drawn up, construction materials had been selected that were inappropriate in appearance and function in the Somontano; the selection awarded fat contracts to their producers, who had friends in the Education Ministry. Nevertheless, such programs, especially those upgrading educational instruction, improving roads, and providing health insurance and pensions, permanently altered the social experience as well as the economic reality of village life.

The reorganization of agricultural production and village life under Franco's regime between 1950 and 1975 represents a shift from preindustrial to industrial capitalism. State reforms determined the timing of the shift, the distribution of its effects, and, indeed, the shift itself. Although Ibieca and the Somontano were not subject to direct state intervention in agriculture, state reforms changed the context in which agriculture was conducted in at least three ways. First, agricultural reforms altered, supplemented, or replaced rural market conditions directly through price controls, guaranteed purchase, tractor sales and rentals, subsidies, and changing terms of credit. Second, they built up the physical and social infrastructure for capitalist farming in the countryside. Third, other reforms reshaped manufacturing in Spain and opened the country to multinational penetration, which in turn affected rural labor, consumer, and producer market conditions. Rather than constituting a program of "planned social change," the reforms orchestrated new conditions to which villagers responded with their own changes in the conduct of agriculture. The reorganization of Somontano agriculture under Franco was certainly a case of state-managed agrarian reform, but one largely mediated by the Invisible Hand of market forces.

❈ Chapter Five
❈ *The Evolution of*
❈ *Capitalist Agriculture*
❈ *in Ibieca*

The barrage of agrarian reforms decreed by the Franco regime during the 1950s and 1960s restructured the context of agriculture in Ibieca. In the 1950s the principal policies and programs affecting Ibieca were those that stabilized the cereals market and sent a limited number of tractors to the provinces for rental and sale. In the 1960s the equipment and supplies to mechanize agriculture, and the credit with which to buy them, became readily available to larger landowners in the Somontano. At the same time, expanding urban labor markets were increasing the work options of poorer families. In the 1970s consumer credit and educational opportunities expanded in the countryside, further restructuring the present and future of village life.

The villagers of Ibieca changed the way they conducted agriculture and organized household economies in response to this evolving context. This chapter describes the reorganization process, first in terms of some of the quantifiable trends that composed it—changes in the employment of labor and machines, in crop and livestock production, in population and land distribution, and in wage work and sources of income. These trends were the combined results of actions of villagers, of the productive strategies described in the second part of the chapter. We shall see how peasants and *amos* have become farmers and how, in changing themselves, they have transformed the social organization of production and the economic bases of social life in the village.

The Reorganization of Production

Mechanization

In the early 1950s, when the Ministry of Agriculture began to sell more tractors in the countryside and the Official Council of Agrarian Unions (COSA) began its tractor rental program, larger landowners were prepared by several market circumstances to buy and hire tractors to work their land. Many large owners had accumulated sizable savings from black market traffic during the 1940s, and between 1950 and 1952 they experienced a precipitous drop in income from crop sales as a result of the closing of the black market.[1] In addition, in the early 1950s agricultural wages in Ibieca began to soar relative to the inflation rate, whereas the two had more or less kept pace during the 1940s. Between 1950 and 1955 a *jornalero's* daily wage increased 250 percent, while inflation increased only 14 percent. (See Table 3, Appendix.)

The agricultural incomes of large landowners, who relied most on wage labor and had profited most from the black market, were most affected by these changing conditions. Large owners had also accumulated the largest savings from the black market which they might invest in mechanization. When the COSA program began in 1952, Ibieca's largest landowners immediately petitioned for tractors to come to Ibieca and plow their fields in place of *mozos* and mules. Luis Solano, Juan Blanco, Fernando Segarra, Tomás Coronas, and Ricardo Sánchez were among those who hired the COSA tractors early on. Later, as these men bought their own tractors, medium and smaller landowners hired the COSA tractors. COSA did not intend to instruct the Somontanese in the virtues of tractor farming; rather, its mandate was to secure the wheat harvest and, through good works, to promote Franco's regime in the countryside. However, the program had tremendous educational effects. A tractor did the work of several men in a fraction of the time, and yields increased because more moisture was available to the roots when the tractor's plow dug deeper into the soil than did the mule's plow.

1. Marti, "Agriculture and Politics," pp. 1–2.

Luis Solano bought Ibieca's first tractor in 1948. It was a 1920 model, one of the original Ford tractors, and did little more than provide novelty for Ibieca's landscape. Five more tractors were bought by Ibieca landowners between 1953 and 1958, all of them ultimately adjudicated through the Ministry of Agriculture, and they began to change the conduct of village agriculture. *Caciquismo* skewed tractor sales in those years, as it had cereal quotas in the 1940s, so that the wealthiest and most influential landowners paid less for their new tractors than less prominent landowners paid for used ones. Luis Solano's first modern tractor was bought used for 70,000 pesetas from a friend in another village; the friend himself had bought it new for half that from the Ministry of Agriculture. In 1955 Solano bought a new tractor from the Ministry of Agriculture for 40,000 pesetas. By 1958 Tomás Coronas and Ricardo Sánchez, both large landowners, and Gabriel Abadía, who rented the Costa estate, had all bought used tractors from private owners for 'rices ranging from 50,000 to 125,000 pesetas.

During the 1960s, as tractors and easy agrarian credit became commercially available, more landowners traded in their mules for tractors. Between 1960 and 1975 villagers bought twenty tractors, about half of them with loans and the rest with savings and trade-ins. Some were purchased to replace old tractors, others by new owners, and a couple as second tractors. In the late 1960s some of the tractor owners bought combines—again, about half of them with agrarian loans. By 1975 ten men owned twelve tractors and five combines and used them to perform virtually all of Ibieca's agricultural work. Agriculture was fully mechanized by then, but villagers did not stop buying tractors—some bought their first tractors, and old tractor owners bought newer and bigger models. The latest-model tractor of the 1950s had around 25 horsepower and its legal-market price was 100,000 pesetas new, whereas the latest model in Ibieca in 1975 had 70 horsepower and cost 500,000 pesetas new.

Crops and Livestock

As landowners mechanized and adapted to changing labor, crop, and livestock markets, they gradually altered their patterns of

Harvesting with the collectively owned combine

land use and animal husbandry. In the long run, small and large landowners alike vastly expanded their production for sale and drastically cut their production for home consumption.

Between 1950 and 1975 the area of village territory planted in olive trees and vines decreased, the area in almond trees stayed the same, and the area in cereals increased dramatically. Between 1955 and 1965 there were about 400 hectares of land in cereals, of which some 250 hectares were cultivated each year. By 1974 700 hectares were in cereals, including over 600 cultivated each year. The area cultivated more than doubled, and there was a two- to threefold increase in yields, so the average annual production in cereals increased more than fourfold. Estimated average annual cereal production in the early 1950s was 100,000 to 150,000 kilograms. In the early 1970s annual production had risen to 600,000 kilograms.[2]

The enormous expansion of cereal production and the other changes in land use during this period occurred in two phases. During the first, which ended in the late 1960s, villagers used their new

2. Mariano Castillo was the source of the estimate for the early 1950s. The figure for the early 1970s is the average production for a three-year period, 1972-74, as reported to the Servico Nacional de Productos Agrarios by villagers.

Table 5. Crop Areas in Ibieca, 1956 and 1974

Crop	1956 (Hectares)	1974 (Hectares)
Cultivated in Cereals	260	600
Fallow Cereal Land	160	100
Total Cereal Land	420	700
Orchards and Vineyards	200	145
Gardens and Forage Crops	5	50
Total Cultivated	625	895
Total Uncultivated	800	575

Source: Based on 1956 cadaster and on Diputación Provincial de Huesca, *Estudio socioeconómico*. Figures are rounded off.

machinery largely within existing patterns of production. The principal trends were a substantial increase in cereal yields and a modest contraction in the area devoted to vineyards. During the second phase, which began in the mid-1960s and was still in progress in 1975, the landscape of Ibieca was visibly transformed by the expansion and reorganization of production. Every year villagers cleared and plowed more scrub oak and fallow and orchard lands and sowed them in cereals. The land cultivated in cereals increased over the years by 300 hectares. Finally, after 1967 cereal production shifted from wheat to barley in response to shifts in official prices of these commodities. In 1967 only 10 percent of the cereal cultivated in Ibieca was barley; by 1975 over half was barley. Table 5 summarizes the trends.

In 1950 Ibieca's agricultural economy was based on multiple crops; by 1975 it was largely based on cereals. What were some of the factors behind the shift? After mechanization, the man-hours required to sow and harvest cereals plummeted by nearly 90 percent, from 180 to 20 man-hours a year. (See Table 6.) The demand for labor in preharvest work in vineyards and orchards also dropped by 20 percent (see Table 7) because villagers could use tractors to turn over the soil. However, demand for labor to harvest olives, almonds, and grapes was not affected. Total demand per hectare for those crops continued to be in the range of 150 to 215 man-hours per year.

Table 6. Labor Required by Various Methods of Cereal Production

Methods	Preharvest Man-hours	Harvest Man-hours	Total Man-hours
Sickle, Threshing Sled, and Pitchfork	74	108	182
Reaper and Thresher	74	63	137
Small Tractor and Thresher	19	26	45
Medium Tractor and Combine	14	6	20

Source: Figures in Ministerio de Agricultura, *Coeficientes horarios,* and my own calculations.

Table 7. Labor Required and Value Added for Crops in Ibieca, 1974

Crop	Man-hours/ Hectare/Year before Mechanization	Man-hours/ Hectare/Year after Mechanization	Value Added/ Man-hour Hectare
Cereals	137–82	20	394
Vines	213	170	141
Olive Trees	266	213	76
Almond Trees	192	154	159

Source: See Table 6 note. Value-added figures derived from data in Diputación Provincial de Huesca, *Estudio socioeconómico.*

After mechanization the "value added" by each man-hour of labor for cereals was about four times that added by each man-hour of labor applied to orchards or vineyards.

Other reasons why cereals took over the land of Ibieca are summarized in Table 8. Cereals could be counted on to yield a reasonably good crop each year, given fertilizer and deep plowing. Their market was reliable and prices were good, given state intervention. They were fully mechanized, required no processing, and the entire

Table 8. Conditions of Crop Production in Ibieca, Early 1970s

Condition or Feature	Cereals	Grapes	Olives	Almonds
Labor requirements				
in pre-harvest work	low	moderate	moderate	moderate
in harvest work	low	high	high	high
Reliability of Crop	high	low	low	low
Processing	no	yes	yes	no
Home Consumption	no	yes	yes	no
Market Condition	good	poor	fair	good

crop could be sold. In contrast, vineyards and olive and almond orchards all required considerable labor, especially during harvest, and
they were relatively unreliable, producing good crops only every
two or three years on the average. Almonds had the advantage of
requiring no processing; furthermore, they were entirely sold on the
market, which until recently provided a reasonably steady and good
price. Olives and grapes, on the other hand, required considerable
processing. The fatal development for first grapes and then olives
was that, for most landowners, the costs of producing them and
making them into wine and oil increased faster than their market
value and the price of store-bought wine and olive oil.

Mechanization and market shifts were also taking their toll on
village livestock. By 1970 only a half-dozen burros remained in the
village. Within a few years, after running water was installed and
they were no longer needed to carry water from the fountain to the
house, all of them were sold. Most families also stopped raising
small livestock (chickens, hens, rabbits, and pigeons) in their stables, and by the late 1970s even household pig-raising was disappearing. Although they were ceasing to produce their own, villagers
ate more pork, chicken, and eggs. They bought the meat in general
stores in the village, which bought it from warehouses in Huesca,
which bought it from livestock factories in the Somontano, including Ibieca. *Granjas*, or livestock factories, mass produced eggs,
chickens, and pigs. They spread rapidly throughout Spain during the
1960s in response to the growing demand for meat and heavy foreign investment by international feed companies.

The first *granja* in Ibieca was set up in the late 1960s by a man from Huesca. It housed 50,000 hens which produced 30,000 eggs a day that were shipped to Huesca. At about the same time, Ramón Loriente from Ibieca set up a pig *granja*. The venture failed, and he was bought out by another family who made it a success. In 1965 Andrés Castro converted the Castro house on the plaza, once one of the biggest and finest in Ibieca, into a chicken *granja*. In 1973 two more livestock *granjas* were built: another one for hens by the man from Huesca, and one for chickens in another big old house near Castro's that the Lacasa brothers bought and converted.

Most mass pig and chicken producers in the Somontano worked under contract with feed companies and slaughterhouses in Huesca. The largest operations in the province were owned by two cousins, Lorenzo and Alejandro Salas. Both men dealt on national markets, and Lorenzo's operation was associated with a multinational feed company, Protector. In 1975 the Lacasa brothers had a typical contract with Lorenzo Salas, who had some 500 *granjas* franchised in the Somontano. Salas supplied the Lacasas with 4,000 baby chickens and two months feed on credit five times a year. The Lacasas supplied the chicken house and the labor involved in raising 20,000 chickens a year. The Lacasas took each two-month-old batch to Salas, who paid them a guaranteed minimum price per kilogram, minus the original costs. If the market price was over the minimum, Salas and the Lacasas split the difference per kilogram. Without putting out any liquid capital, the Lacasas sold an estimated 1.25 million pesetas (nearly $20,000) worth of chickens to Salas in 1973-74. The risk was, of course, that a batch of chickens would die, due to disease or some other catastrophe, in which case the Lacasas would be in debt to Salas for the original costs.

Sheep raising was transformed from a wool-producing to a meat-producing activity by 1975, but its organization was not industrialized. The price of wool actually fell after 1960, from 50 pesetas to 23 pesetas per kilogram, but it was still high enough so that its sale covered the cost of shearing. Transhumance was abandoned with the shift from wool to meat because it interfered with the capacity of sheep to produce meat. When pastured year around in Ibieca, sheep attained full natural weight, their diet could be supplemented with feed to fatten them more, and they gave birth to two lambs (instead of one) a year.

Solano's flock had 270 sheep in 1971, only 20 more than in the mid-1950s. The collective flock grew considerably; 350-400 sheep were owned by ten to fifteen houses in the mid-1950s, whereas 775 were owned by twenty-eight houses in 1971. Many small landholding houses bought a few sheep during the 1960s, and the Rivera brothers added about 250 sheep around 1970. Mariano Castillo, the treasurer of the collective flock, estimated that gross income from the sale of lambs from both flocks in 1971 was 1.25 million pesetas, about half of it going to Solano and the Riveras. The expansion was nipped around 1975; sheep owners too were caught in cost squeezes, mainly from soaring shepherd wages and feed prices. Some owners were talking about forming an industrial sheep cooperative that would be eligible for state subsidies and easy credit, while others were selling their sheep.

In 1975 only old-fashioned household pig-raising had survived the tumultuous changes of prior years, although even there the pig's diet and fattening schedule had changed. A pig raised exclusively on potatoes and household scraps took twelve to fourteen months to reach slaughtering weight of 100 to 120 kilograms. A pig raised on a diet supplemented with artificial feed, as all were in the 1970s, took six or seven months to reach the same weight. Economically, pig-raising was still attractive—in 1971 it cost a family 5,000 pesetas to buy and raise a piglet, and its products, *mondongo* and cured meat, were worth 10,000 pesetas. The main reason why pig-raising survived so long, however, was probably because it had a social role in animating core kin, friendship, and neighbor networks, and because it provided women with gifts to exchange.

Migration and Land Ownership

During the 1950s there were a dozen landless households in Ibieca; by 1965 none remained. Small landowning families also left. Ibieca's total population declined from 300 to 150 between 1950 and 1975. Of the some forty families that stayed in Ibieca, many younger adults, including the heirs to a dozen estates who once would have made their lives in the village, migrated to cities and returned only for visits. Finally, there was some "hidden migration" in that many of the young men and women who continued to live in the village drove to jobs in Huesca or nearby factories each weekday. For them the village had become a suburb, a bedroom community.

The decline in population was precipitous, but it did not over-reach the labor saved by mechanization. In 1955 there were eighty-nine males age 15 to 65 in Ibieca, and in 1972 there were thirty-nine. The number of man-hours required to cultivate cereal, olive, almond, and grape crops during those years decreased at almost ex-actly the same pace, from 87,000 to 39,800, even though land under cultivation increased by some 300 hectares.[3]

The distribution of land was fairly stable throughout the period because migrant landowners did not sell their estates when they left. (See Table 9; see Appendix, Table 4 for comparable data on Aragon.) In the half-dozen sales that did occur, owners either sold only the land and kept the house for weekend and summer visits, or they sold the house and the land separately. Neither altered the overall pattern much. Enterprising farming families added the land to their holdings, and city dwellers, usually with kin in Ibieca, bought the houses for vacations.

Several forces militated against owners selling their lands in the 1970s. The continuity of the *casa* was grounded in landownership, which consequently symbolized security and prestige. Moreover, land prices were soaring, especially during the 1970s. According to Juan García, a cereal field he bought in 1974 for 35,000 pesetas a hectare would fetch at least 100,000 pesetas in 1979, and he said he would not sell it for less than twice that.

Property was being consolidated in two ways short of land trans-fers. Sharecropping, which in effect transferred control over land from large to small owners, virtually disappeared during the 1960s. Land renting by the owners of tractors and combines increased, es-pecially during the 1970s, which consolidated de facto control over village properties of all sizes in the hands of large owners. In addi-tion, landowners were consolidating their own plots, sometimes merely joining adjacent plots of their own, sometimes swapping plots with the owner of a neighboring field. Juan García owned a field in the middle of one owned by Juan Solano, for example, and Solano proposed that García trade his field for another of his own choosing. García agreed, picked a field, and they signed a contract to that effect in the village secretary's office. By such mergers and ex-

3. The 1955 figure is my own calculation. The 1972 figure is from Diputación Provincial de Huesca, *Estudio socioeconómico.*

Table 9. Land Distribution in Ibieca, 1960 and 1972

	Number of Land Owners	
	1960	1972
Minifundia (under 3 hectares)	10	8
Small Estates (3–10 hectares)	23	19
Medium Estates (10–30 hectares)	13	12
Large Estates (30–100 hectares)	10	11
Latifundia (over 100 hectares)	1	1
Total	57	50

Source: Village land records (1960) and 1972 agrarian census published by the Instituto Nacional de Estadístico. Figures on property distribution in Aragon in Biescas, *Economía aragonesa*, p. 112, show that the proportion of small holders decreased by 8.5 percent between 1962 and 1972, though the proportion of land they held remained constant.

changes the number of fields in Ibieca was reduced from nearly 800 in 1962 to less than 400 in 1972.

Wage Work and Income

As we have seen in previous chapters, villagers have always augmented their income from agricultural production with income from other sources, especially from wage labor, trades, and shops. Income from other sources continued to be as important, perhaps more important, in sustaining village households during the transition to more advanced capitalist agriculture. In the early 1970s about thirty men and women in Ibieca held salaried jobs. A dozen men were employed more or less full-time in agriculture as fieldhands and tractor drivers; there were also four shepherds, a state road repairman, and fifteen young unmarried men and women who held a variety of jobs in Huesca or nearby towns. Some of the latter lived with relatives in the town or city where they worked during the week and came home to Ibieca on weekends, while others commuted every day.

A half-dozen men were self-employed in more or less full-time nonagricultural occupations. Ramón Blanco owned a bar, and Mariano Castillo and Juan Lacasa each owned general stores. The business of both stores and the bar mushroomed in recent years and, with it, the income they produced. Tomás and José Lacasa ran the bakery, which served a half-dozen surrounding villages as well as Ibieca, and Ramón Lacasa was a semi-independent truckdriver. Finally, three bricklayers, Miguel Miranda and his two sons, worked full-time modernizing old-fashioned houses.

A vast array of minor or seasonal sources of income were available. Day laborers, mostly men, were still hired to harvest olives and almonds during the late fall. In the case of olives, if the laborer had no trees, a kind of sharecropping arrangement was common in which he was paid in a share of the crop. One man sheared sheep; two others pruned trees and vines; another ran a vegetable hothouse. At least three women served on a part-time or occasional basis and washed clothes for other houses. Two young women worked a couple of hours a day packing the eggs laid in the hen *granja*. A dozen villagers went to a hotspring resort in the Catalan Pyrenees each summer to work as maids, dishwashers, garbagemen, pastrymakers, and waitresses.

A half-dozen villagers were paid fees by the state for service rendered: a town crier, a telephone operator, a mailman, a bill and tax collector, and a man who distributed pensions and social security. The state paid elderly villagers more in pensions and social security than it collected in taxes. In 1973 Angela Iglesias received about 6,000 pesetas from the state as her pension; she, in turn, paid about one-tenth that amount in property taxes (*contribución*) to the village government and another tenth for municipal upkeep of the village television and for spraying village olive and almond groves with sulfates.

Table 10 presents the estimated average wages for the salaried jobs in Ibieca in the early 1970s. In 1953, an unskilled agricultural worker earned 5,500 pesetas in Ibieca, and the cost of living tripled between 1953 and 1973. (See Table 3, Appendix.) Thus real wages for unskilled agricultural workers increased by a magnitude of five and a half between 1953 and 1973, when the yearly salary was 90,000 pesetas.

Since about half of the houses in the village had one or more salaried working members, those households were earning 90,000

Table 10. Estimated Average Salaries in Ibieca, Early 1970s

	Salary	
Job	Pesetas	Dollars
Unskilled Agricultural Worker	90,000	1385
Skilled Agricultural Worker	150,000	2308
Semi-Skilled City Worker	200,000	3077
Teacher	250,000	3846

Source: Salaries quoted by villagers.

pesetas or more beyond income from the sale of crops and livestock. In the case of small landholding houses, income from wages was substantially larger than the 60,000 pesetas typically earned from crops. Also, all small and medium landholders availed themselves of one or more of the minor or seasonal sources of income, adding another few thousand pesetas a year.

Of all crops, cereals produced the largest and most widely distributed increase in income. For the village as a whole, real cereal income tripled or quadrupled between the early 1950s and the early 1970s.[4] How much a particular household increased its cereal income depended on how much more land it had put into cereals and how much it invested in producing higher yields. Mariano Castillo surpassed others in both respects, increasing his real income by five and a half times between the early 1950s and 1971. The price of almonds increased enough to keep ahead of production costs during the period, but not enough to produce an increase in real income— and, in any case, the income was not widely distributed. Olives produced income by saving the cost of purchased olive oil, but the "income" thus produced declined as the production cost approached the purchase cost. After cereals, and more than olives or almonds, livestock has increased real agricultural incomes in Ibieca

4. The increase in real income was calculated by multiplying official cereal prices by the cereal surpluses of the 1950s estimated by Mariano Castillo, and by the 1971 SNPA figures on cereal production in the village. This figure was then divided by the rise in provincial cost of living, information on which was provided by the provincial Instituto Nacional de Estadístico.

Table 11. Crop and Livestock Incomes in Ibieca, 1974

Crop and Livestock	Millions of Pesetas
Cereals	5.0
Olives and Almonds	2.9
Other Crops	2.5
Total Gross Crop Income	10.4
Livestock	2.9
Total Gross Crop and Livestock Income	13.3
Depreciation and Property Taxes	1.5
Net Agricultural Income	11.8

Source: Diputación Provincial de Huesca, *Estudio socioeconómico.*

in recent years. In the case of *granjas* the effects are limited to a few houses, whereas in the case of sheep most houses have partaken in the increased incomes.

According to 1974 estimates, cereals produced about half of Ibieca's gross crop income. (See Table 11.) For small landholding houses without almond trees or livestock factories, cereals produced as much as or more than half of their agricultural income.

Although types of land held were not uniform, Table 12 gives us a rough idea of the average agricultural income in each landholding category. Large landholders made ten times the agricultural income of small and poor landholders, and Casa Solano, the largest landholder, made sixty times more. However, wages paid are not included in these figures, so some portion of the income of large and very large landholders was redistributed to small and poor landholders in the form of wages. In 1975, for example, Juan Solano paid nearly a third of his gross income out in wages for his agricultural and domestic workers. On the other hand, small landowners also transferred some of their income to large landowners in exchange for machine time.

The flow of money into Ibieca from crops, livestock, jobs, shops, and social security increased tremendously during the 1950s, 1960s, and 1970s. Some of the increase was offset by higher costs of production. Costs increased most for the large and medium landholders who owned agricultural machinery, but those people also made

Table 12. Estimated Gross Agricultural Incomes in Ibieca, 1974

Landholding Group	N	Average Agricultural Income	
		Pesetas	Dollars
Small Estates and Minifundia	27	61,000	940
Medium Estates	12	167,000	2,570
Large Estates	11	473,000	7,280
Latifundia	1	2,954,000	45,450

Source: See Table 11, note. N is from 1972 agrarian census: income distribution was calculated on the basis of 1960 figures, since the 1972 census did not include data on the amount of land per landholding category.

proportionately more profit. Small holders did not experience higher costs—indeed, they may have had lower costs—until the end of the 1960s, when they started buying chemical fertilizers and forage crops for their sheep.

Based on the calculations above, disposable income, or income minus production costs, increased ten to fifteen times in money terms and three to five times in real terms. Judging from figures on savings accounts in the Provincial Rural Savings Bank, a lot of the new money was saved: between 1966 and 1975 savings accounts increased from 28 million to 3.3 billion pesetas.[5] Some of the new income was spent on food and goods that villagers had once produced themselves but had stopped producing. And, beginning in the late 1960s, villagers spent some of their increased income to improve their material living conditions and to enhance their children's futures. They mechanized and renovated their houses, installing fully modern bathrooms, butane stoves, washing machines, and refrigerators. They bought televisions, motorbikes, and cars. Many children, some from the poorest houses, were continuing their educations beyond the required age of fourteen, learning technical and clerical skills and earning teaching certificates and professional degrees.

Although the custom of saving money was nothing new in Ibieca,

5. Caja Rural Provincial de Huesca, *Memoria*.

the custom of spending it voluntarily and in good conscience was entirely new. It was one thing to learn to spend money regularly on productive resources and food, but quite another to learn to spend it on material and social "improvements." Villagers were becoming increasingly involved in the consumer market and seeking the means of upward mobility for their children. They had come to accept as an enduring reality what must have seemed at first risky and fickle bonanza; furthermore, they had committed themselves to reproducing a new world, not to continuing the one that produced them.

Family Farming Strategies

In 1950 small landowners and landless laborers did most of the agricultural work of the village, working their own lands and those of large landowners as sharecroppers, hired hands, and day laborers. In 1975 the agricultural work of the village was done by large landowners with tractors and combines, working their own lands and those of others. The time devoted to agricultural labor was cut in half, while the amount of land under cultivation in cereals increased by 130 percent, and cereal production and real household incomes increased by 400 percent. Half the village was gone, and the organization of agricultural work was turned upside down. The villagers who remained were no longer peasants, laborers, and *amos*. Ibieca in 1975 was composed of farming families.

Because most of these trends were wrought via market mechanisms, Ibieca's transformation appears to be a straightforward case of capitalist development—the unfolding of a process with an internal logic of its own. The transformation was indeed a case of developing agrarian capitalism, but its logic was not internal. Rather, its form and pace, and even the fact that it occurred at all, ultimately resulted from state policies. The first tractors used in Ibieca in the 1950s were rented and purchased from state agencies, and much of the agricultural machinery purchased later was funded by special state-controlled agrarian loans and state subsidies. The cereals market, which provided so much of the incentive for mechanization and the remaking of the village landscape during the 1960s and

1970s, was state managed and manipulated. The production of cereals in Ibieca increased as the price of cereals and other supports rose. When the price hikes and supports favored barley over wheat, villagers shortly sowed more barley and less wheat.

The agrarian reforms were indirect, involving little or no active intervention by state agents, but they were very powerful, very compelling. Other circumstances wrought by the state and by history contributed to the transformation by in some way releasing villagers to act more autonomously. The Civil War and anarchist revolution, for example, had already turned their world upside down, calling into question once and for all the authority of the *amos* and of God. The power of both was restored, but the illusion of their invulnerability was not. During the 1940s the black market enticed most village families into an illicit scramble for money that betrayed their more modest conventional mores and expectations. Finally, the heavy hand of political repression under Franco meant that *amos* had no political stake in labor-intensive agricultural techniques that maximized the number of votes they might control through the work process. Suspending elections, in effect, suspended an important source of resistance to mechanization for village *amos*.

During the 1950s and 1960s, as peasants and *amos* responded to state agrarian reforms, they converted themselves into farmers and dissolved two forms of production (early capitalist and peasant) into one capitalist form. The *amos* converted first; during the 1950s they rented and then purchased tractors to work their land. Most of the landless laboring families had migrated to cities by the early 1960s, leaving the dwindling agricultural wage work to peasant families. Some peasant families had hired tractors from the beginning, and during the 1960s more and more converted, hiring their former bosses to plow their land and harvest their cereals for an hourly fee.

By 1975 all the families in Ibieca were farming families in several senses. All owned land which they farmed themselves or arranged for others to farm. They mechanized as much of the work as they could and minimized manual labor. Most of their agricultural production was for market sale, and most of what they consumed was purchased rather than homegrown. Market forces had taken control of their decisions about what to produce and how to produce it.

Such decisions and relations had less emphasis on social and more on economic ramifications. Villagers had learned "how to maximize returns and minimize expenditures, to buy cheap and sell dear, regardless of social obligations and social costs."[6] In so doing they had converted agriculture from a way of life into a livelihood.

Both peasant and early capitalist production had generated multidimensional social relations that were laden with reciprocal obligations. Those obligations were balanced among peasants and unequal between *amos* and their laborers, but both sorts constituted an experience of connection and interdependence. In relation to the connections that once linked Ibieca's rich and poor families, the connections between farmers and their workers and the tractor-hiring arrangements were spare and instrumental, lacking in both social ramifications and political weight.

The relationship between mechanized farmers and their workers still echoed the old understandings; it was not a mere exchange of wages for labor. Andrés Castro and Juan Solano still called on the other members of their workers' families for extra labor—for example, a worker's wife might be called to cook on a feast day, or to assist in making *mondongo*. However, by 1975 bosses paid for extra labor. It was not theirs by right, and in general the relationship was free of extraneous expectations. As Lorenzo Lobera put it, "Nobody does anything for nothing anymore." The promise of favors and access to other jobs and resources with which *amos* could once hold their laborers meant little by 1975. Workers' kinsmen who migrated to cities developed their own lines of access; the availability of loans and jobs had increased generally; state health insurance and social security programs cared for them in sickness and old age. Village agricultural workers still used the term *amo* to describe their bosses, but its meaning had changed. It had come to denote an employer, not a master.

Joint ownership of tractors and combines, and arrangements between farmers who owned the machines and those who hired them to work their lands, also echoed old understandings, more from resource-sharing among peasant families than from *amo*/laborer relations. The idiom in which the arrangements were made was a

6. Wolf, *Peasant Wars*, p. 279.

neighborly one, often found among families related by blood or marriage. Tomás Coronas said he and his son worked the lands of their friends and relatives as a favor, not because of the modest fee they earned, and he avoided calling it a rental arrangement. (In 1978 an hour of tractor time cost 400 pesetas, while the daily wage for a skilled agricultural worker was 1,000 pesetas.) Nevertheless, the fee was paid on a strict hourly basis, and because fees were not keeping pace with costs in the late 1970s the owners of agricultural machinery, including Coronas, began to withdraw from their agreements to work their neighbors and kinsmen's land on an hourly basis. Likewise, in discussions of joint-ownership arrangements, there was an uneasy jockeying between profit considerations and the social bonds at stake. Although the idiom of sharing resources had survived, much of its meaning was lost, supplanted by the imperatives of profitmaking.

The agrarian reorganization of the 1950s and 1960s yielded one form of production, capitalist farming, in Ibieca. Two major versions of that form involved the full-time farmers who owned agricultural machinery and the part-time farmers who hired them to plow and harvest their fields. When we examine family histories, more variations come into focus. Some full-time farmers were more entrepreneurial; others seemed to keep one leg in the world of *amos*. Some part-time farmers devoted their spare time to overseeing the work on their lands; others rented their fields and abandoned the pretense of control over the productive process. How a family farmed its land in 1975 depended on circumstances of the family cycle and on the proclivities of family members, as well as on whether the family members were peasants or *amos* in the beginning.

In 1975 three dozen families, mostly small and medium landholders, were part-time farmers. Most of them were otherwise retired from gainful employment, worked for wages, or were engaged in commerce. Briefly, here is how three small landholding families made the transition into farming.

Mariano Castillo, a small landholder who had just married in the mid-1950s, was among the first to hire COSA tractors. Subsequently, he hired Tomás Coronas, his father's first cousin, to work his fields while he expanded his general store. His father, Daniel,

*kept tending their vineyards and orchards until the early 1970s,
when his failing health and market forces convinced Mariano to
uproot the trees and vines and sow the land in cereals. Daniel
agreed to sell his burro in 1973, when the newly installed system of
running water usurped the animal's only remaining function, but
some of his soul seemed to depart with the beast. Over the next
few years, as Mariano streamlined the estate and sent his daughter
to medical school and his son to agronomy school, Daniel gradually stopped talking.*

*During the 1950s Lorenzo Lobera, Antonia Clavero, and their
children were in Sesa, in the south of the province, operating a
small brick factory. Antonia's father, Eugenio, stayed home and
boarded with neighboring families in exchange for labor on their
land. Eugenio also shared a mule team and some small cereal-
harvesting machines with his neighbors. Antonia and Lorenzo returned to Ibieca in 1963, when Eugenio's health no longer permitted him to take care of himself. Within a few years they were hiring
another neighbor to work their land mechanically. Their son, Joaquín, got a job in his uncle's brick factory on the outskirts of the
village; Lorenzo also worked there occasionally. For years both
worked in Juan Solano's olive oil mill during the late winter
months, pressing the olives of all the families in Ibieca and returning the oil to them for a small fee. When the brick factory closed,
Joaquín took a job as a farmhand with Solano and eventually obtained a tractor operator's license. Solano rented his tractor and
combine to Joaquín on Sundays so he could work his own land. In
the late 1970s, with great reluctance and regret, Lorenzo agreed to
let Joaquín uproot their vineyards and orchards in order to sow
more cereals. Lorenzo could no longer work them, and Joaquín had
neither the time nor the devotion to do so.*

*Benito Cuevas and his son, Ismael, worked as hired hands for
Luis Solano during the 1950s. After hours they worked their own
small estate and one they sharecropped. During the cereal harvest
they shared labor, mules, and small machines with Casa Barraca.
Benito died in 1956, and Ismael gave up the sharecropping arrangement and began to work their land with Solano's tractor, which he
rented on Sundays. Ismael married in 1962; three years later he
quit working for Solano, moved to Huesca, and found a factory job.*

Since Ismael Cuevas was an heir, it was an excruciating move for his mother, Angela Iglesias, to endure, but by then he could live in Huesca and still fulfill his obligation to cultivate the estate. In the 1970s Ismael came out to Ibieca on a dozen weekends each year to oversee the farming of his land by Ricardo Sánchez. In spite of her seventy years of age, his mother kept the casa *garden and fruit trees and the* casa *itself (including its anthropological boarder) lively and productive. Angela's oldest daughter lived four houses down the road with her husband and child; her other five children, who live in Huesca and Zaragoza, vacationed in Ibieca with their families during the summer.*

Had Ismael moved to Barcelona or Zaragoza, rather than to Huesca, he would have had to sharecrop or rent his estate because it would have been too far to commute often. By 1970 sharecropping arrangements were rare, and families unable to work their own estates at all rented them to neighbors with agricultural machinery. Small landholders rented their cereal fields and let their orchards and vineyards go to weed or had them uprooted and sown with cereals. Two large landowners rented their entire estates:

When Juan Blanco and his wife sent their son, Ricardo, to law school in Madrid in the 1950s, they hoped he would earn the degree but not use it. They wanted him to return to Ibieca to administer their estate, the second largest in the village. However, he did not return; indeed, he rarely came even for a visit. Juan kept working the estate until 1965, hiring tractors from COSA and then from his neighbors. In 1965 he sharecropped his estate to one family, then another, from neighboring villages. The sharecroppers paid for all the fertilizer, seed, and so on, turning over one-third of the crop to the Blancos. After Juan died in 1970, his widow and sister rented the estate to the Rivera brothers. The Riveras worked the Blanco estate as if it belonged to them and turned over the cash equivalent of one-third of the crops to Gregoria and Juan's sister, Clementina. Since he was a migrant heir who neither oversaw the work on his estate nor visited the community, some of the neighbors guessed that Ricardo would sell the whole patrimony when his mother and aunt died.

Sebastiana Bandrés's parents died in the early 1950s. Andrés Castro then decided to sharecrop his and his wife's sizable estates to Sebastiana's cousins in nearby Aguas. Around 1965 Andrés converted his family house in the plaza, one of the finest houses in the village, into a granja *and devoted himself to raising chickens. A few years later, by then in his sixties, he became dissatisfied with his sharecroppers and decided to work his estates with hired hands. With profits from his* granja *he bought a new tractor on installments and a used binder and thresher. Andrés hired one or two farmhands (elderly ones, so he could pay half-time wages) to help him work his land and run his* granja *for a fixed fee. Andrés had struggled since he was twelve to keep his own, and then also his wife's, estate solvent. He had hoped for a son who would share his entrepreneurial spirit—his dream was to own a half-dozen* granjas*—but he and Sebastiana were childless. Their estates would be passed on to nieces and nephews, who would most likely sell them off piecemeal to their neighbors.*

The difference between overseeing the work on one's own land and renting an estate involved much more than the time and attention invested. Estate owners preferred to hire farmers with machinery to work their land because that way they reaped more of the profit; in addition, some still derived meaning from even peripheral control over the productive process. As we can see from the Blanco and Castro stories, renting also symbolized the last gasp of a *casa*, a step taken because there was no heir to keep it alive. In the mid-1970s a subtle tension was building between farmers who owned agricultural machines and their neighbors who hired them, as the discrepancy between the fees received and the costs of production squeezed machinery owners. They increasingly preferred to rent their neighbors' fields, for the sake of profit and to avoid being bothered with their neighbors' ideas about when and how to plow and reap.

Into this breach stepped Enrique Barrio, the son of a small landowner who had been living in Barcelona for ten years before he returned to Ibieca in 1975. He decided that he preferred farming to running a shop in the city, and he devised a strategy to become a full-time farmer despite his father's modest holdings. Enrique bought a used tractor and, with two other small landowners, a used combine. The production costs of other machinery owners in the village were bloated, in part, because they were buying huge tractors and combines. Enrique bought small ones that could be operated for modest hourly fees. His neighbors who did not want to succumb to renting turned to Enrique when the other machinery owners resisted appeals for their time. Enrique's timing was good in another respect. While not much land had changed hands in the village during the 1950s and 1960s, in the mid-1970s some families who had migrated years before finally put their estates up for sale, so Enrique was able gradually to add to his father's landholdings.

Except for Enrique Barrio and Gabriel Abadía, who rented the Costa estate during the 1950s and 1960s and the Castro estate after 1975, the mechanized farmers were large landowners. All owned at least thirty hectares: Tomás Coronas (43 hectares), Ricardo Sánchez (49), Felipe Barraca (31), Tomás and José Lacasa (30), Luis Segarra (60), Juan Solano (282), Jesús and José Rivera (82), Andrés Castro (57), and Juan García (52).[7] Each followed a different path toward mechanized farming, one shaped as much by considerations of *casa* as by how embroiled they had been in the world of *amos*.

Two of the most entrepreneurially successful farmers, Tomás Coronas and Ricardo Sánchez, owned estates of under 50 hectares— and thus had limited commitments to laboring families. Their family cycles during the 1950s and 1960s also supplied them with father-son work teams.

Tomás Coronas was fifty when he bought his first tractor in 1957. At the same time he dispatched his full-time worker, and his son, Joaquín, left school at twelve to help work their lands. Tomás said he bought a tractor because "it worked more and we worked less." He and Joaquín traded in their tractor for bigger and bigger ones that worked still faster, and in the late 1960s they joined with five neighbors to buy a combine. In 1978 they withdrew from the group

7. These estate sizes were derived from village records which were not updated each year; thus they should be taken as approximations.

combine arrangement, instead purchasing a used combine and a new 75-horsepower tractor. By then the hourly fees were discouraging them from renting to their neighbors, and so were the commercial taxes they owed for renting their machinery. Their entrepreneurial future was cloudy in another respect: Joaquín became engaged in 1979, and he told his father that he and his bride would not be moving into the patrimonial house. They planned to live in Huesca so their children could go to school there and because Joaquín's fiancée's kin lived there. They intended to build a house on the outskirts of Ibieca for use on weekend visits and in the summer; otherwise Joaquín would commute to Ibieca each day to work the family estate. Tomás was deeply angered by his son's plans, which he said were egotistical and immoral. But he also recognized that his son would lose his fiancée otherwise, and that his chances of finding another who would live in Ibieca were very slim. It was Joaquín's fiancée who did not want to live in Ibieca and who insisted that they have their own house when they came for visits. She did not want to live in a world defined by Joaquín's parents, specifically by his mother. Joaquín's mother, who also wished to avoid clashing in-law wills, was obviously as pleased as his father was distressed by it all.

Ricardo Sánchez was twenty-six when he and his father bought their first tractor in 1956. They had already dismissed their full-time worker five years earlier, when Ricardo finished his military service. Explaining why they bought the tractor, Ricardo stressed that the COSA tractors had proven that a tractor would spare them hundreds of hours of arduous labor each year, and that it would increase their yields and income. Not only could they avoid hiring day laborers for all but harvesting, but they could also earn money instead of spending it on wages. In 1957 a tractor fetched 60 pesetas an hour, while a day laborer earned 60 pesetas a day. Like Tomás and Joaquín Coronas, Ricardo bought bigger and bigger tractors, and in the mid-1960s bought his first combine jointly with his wife's brother, who lived in a nearby village. In the late 1970s Ricardo was beginning to turn away offers from his neighbors, who wanted to hire him by the hour, in favor of renting and buying fields. In his mid-forties, he could count on working his estate for another twenty years at least, and it remained to be seen

*whether either of his two adolescent sons would join him and con-
tinue the* casa.

All the mechanized farmers extended themselves entrepreneurially, with Coronas and Sánchez the most aggressive in hiring themselves out to their neighbors. Others built *granjas* and developed
their livestock enterprises. The two most entrepreneurial families,
the Lacasas and the Riveras, whom villagers described as "animating" Ibieca, were relative newcomers to large-scale farming and
therefore had no lingering attachments to the world of *amos*.

*Julian Lacasa and Engracia Bierge both inherited small estates
which they combined when they married in 1920. With the assis-
tance of four sons, they sharecropped additional land for the next
thirty years. In the late 1940s they were able to send their second
son, Juan, to Monzón for a year's apprenticeship in a bakery, and
then to help him set up a bakery in Ibieca with his brothers. Over
the next decade the Lacasa brothers displaced village women as
bakers, in Ibieca and in a half-dozen surrounding communities. In
1960 Juan withdrew from the fraternal partnership and opened a
general store with his wife. In 1967 Ramón, the youngest son, married, moved to Huesca, bought a truck, and became an olive oil
agent for Aceites Calvo. Ramón's wife inherited a 20-hectare estate
which his brothers, Tomás and José, managed. In 1971 Tomás and
José bought the Toro estate, doubling their landholdings, and a
tractor. In 1975 they set up a chicken* granja *in the Rios house, next
door to Andrés Castro's* casa/granja *on the central plaza. Julian
Lacasa's sons will likely divide the properties and go their own
ways after his death. In the meantime, his long life and the fact
that his eldest son and designated heir, José, remained a bachelor
in his fifties have forestalled the usual splits among brothers.*

*The Rivera brothers' story is likewise one of diversifying invest-
ments, but at a faster clip. They were living in Huesca and working
in their father's bakery when he inherited Bernardo Costa's 46-
hectare estate in 1960. Gabriel Abadía had been renting Costa's
estate since shortly after the Civil War, and the Riveras continued
the arrangement. They bought Abadía a tractor in 1960, and in
1969 they purchased a share in the combine collective. In 1970 the*

four Rivera brothers started to work their land themselves, as well as Juan Blanco's 84-hectare estate, which they rented from his widow. They also rented, and in 1976 bought, Fernando Badía's 36 hectares. Within a few years they owned 250 sheep in the village sheep collective, started two pig granjas, and built an irrigation system for their forage crops. The Rivera brothers did all of this without moving to Ibieca—they commuted every day. After most of the enterprises were launched, two of the brothers dropped out and took factory jobs in Huesca. Jesús and José Rivera were still commuting to Ibieca daily in the late 1970s, and both had built substantial weekend houses on the village outskirts.

All of the Lacasa brothers' entrepreneurialism was accomplished without hiring wage workers, and much of the Riveras' was, too. In the late 1970s the Riveras were hiring several village men on a part-time basis—the equivalent of about one full-time worker. Clearly, sheer zeal was one source of Lacasa and Rivera expansionism, but the fact that they could draw on family labor (in the form of two to four brothers) and on non-agricultural capital (a bakery in both cases) actually enabled them to exercise that zeal. Their vision and latitude was, furthermore, uncluttered by the *amo* experience. In each of these respects the Riveras and the Lacasas distinguish themselves from Luis Segarra and Juan Solano.

Before the Civil War, Fernando Segarra reassembled the estate his uncle and aunt had dismembered. By 1950 he had assumed a prominent position in village politics, serving as mayor for most of the previous decade. His casa owned two mule teams and hired two full-time laborers, two servants, and occasional day laborers. Just before Fernando's death in 1952, a friend in the Ministry of Agriculture offered him an adjudicated tractor for 22,000 pesetas, not much more than the cost of a pair of mules. Fernando declined the offer. His son, Luis, who was twenty-eight at the time, did not know why his father declined it, but he was not in a hurry to mechanize, either. Luis hired COSA tractors during the 1950s, and later he hired Gabriel Abadía to plow his land. In 1973 he finally bought his own tractor. He was among those who bought a share of the group combine in 1969, when he dismissed his full-time work-

ers, and in 1979 he still owned that share. Luis did not really care about cereals or machines, nor did profit inspire him greatly. He tended his vineyards and orchards long past their commercial prime, for the sake of having wine and oil from his land on the family table, and his heart was in his herd of milk cows. The herd was no doubt a reasonable enterprise in the 1950s, and probably still in the 1960s, but in the 1970s the price of the milk he sold to villagers fell considerably behind his production costs and the value of his labor. Luis let his workers go, mechanized his farming, and worked long hours at manual labor—all modifications or departures from the amo role. The fact that he neither possessed nor aspired to a political voice in the village was another departure. The echoes of the amo role were in his sluggishness—and his father's refusal—to mechanize, and in his devotion to relatively unremunerative activities that kept his casa in touch with the land and with the village. It was unclear whether Luis's son would continue the estate, let alone transform it. In 1979, at 18, he was attending college.

Juan Solano owned Ibieca's other herd of cows. His estate was four to five times larger than those of the other large landowners in Ibieca, and he and his father were considerably quicker than the Segarras to avail themselves of new techniques and options. At the same time, they too cleaved to some amo ends and means. Juan was making even less profit from his herd than was Luis Segarra, since Juan paid a full-time cowherd to pasture it; but the herd kept his casa connected to other families, as dozens of villagers came to his house every day to buy milk. Casa Solano employed a dozen full-time laborers and servants in the 1940s, and during harvests it hired dozens more as day laborers. The casa owned four pairs of mules, which Juan and his father, Luis, gradually replaced with tractors during the 1950s and 1960s. They kept most of their workers on during the 1950s in order to clear a huge tract of scrub oak north of the village. A hundred hectares, it took eight years to clear before it could be planted in cereal. A few of Solano's neighbors watched the project with some resentment because they thought that the tract was not entirely his, that some of it belonged to the village. Solano's neighbors also described in some detail the subsi-

dies and nearly interest-free loans he had obtained from his friends in the Ministry of Agriculture in order to pay for clearing the land.

A hundred hectares of cereal was a vast expanse—about a quarter of all the village land sown in cereals at the time. As the sharecropping arrangements on his vineyards and olive orchards lapsed, Solano recovered them during the 1960s and converted some into more cereal fields and almond orchards. Profit seems to have motivated Solano to remake the landscape of his estate, but he could not or did not want to change his heavy commitment to wage labor, which continued to take a large bite out of his casa *income. In 1975 he hired on a yearly basis four full-time agricultural workers, one part-time worker, and a part-time domestic servant. He could not cut back more on his hiring without eliminating some productive activities, nor could he expand much without hiring more workers. In the late 1970s he established a cattle* granja *across the road from his house, one small enough not to require a full-time worker's attention. No doubt it added to his income, but it was neither an efficient operation nor an especially lucrative investment. Solano's sheep flock was the same size as the Rivera brothers' flock, but less profitable, because Solano paid a shepherd's full wage while the Riveras shared shepherd and pasture costs with the owners of the other 500 sheep in the village flock.*

Juan Solano kept his olive oil mill open each winter through the 1960s, even though the fees he charged barely covered the wages he paid Lorenzo and Joaquín Lobera to run it. He did not like to give up a productive activity until he lost money from it. For example, he still maintained large olive orchards, and he let two-thirds of his olive crop rot on the trees because day labor for the harvest would have cost more than the olives were worth. Many other large owners did likewise, but the Rivera brothers managed to pick their entire crop with family labor and neighborly exchanges. That year half of the olives pressed in Solano's mill, at cost and possibly at a loss to him, belonged to the Riveras. As Solano watched them unload wagon after wagon of olives, the tension in the mill became palpable. Seeing the Riveras profit at his expense visibly irked Solano, and that was the last year he operated the mill. By 1975 he had replaced the press with a feed-grain mill to supply his cattle.

His oldest son was thirteen and able to run the grain mill with the help of his younger brother. Juan Solano's four sons held out the promise of a future for his casa—*but only the promise.*

Father and son worked alongside one another during the 1950s and 1960s in Casa Castillo, Casa Coronas, and Casa Sánchez, while the Rivera and Lacasa brothers teamed up to reorient their productive activities. The family cycles of Casa Castro, Casa Blanco, Casa Segarra, and Casa Solano either provided no such family labor team, or it was short-circuited by death or migration. These were the four largest landowning houses in the village, and in one way or another each seemed stymied by its heritage as *amos*. Juan Blanco sent his only son to law school thinking he would return and administer the family estate. Andrés Castro and Luis Segarra were slow to take up mechanized farming. Juan Solano's business acumen might have made him a good *amo*, but it did not serve him very well as a capital-intensive farmer.

The families who most aggressively and effectively transformed Ibieca were on lower rungs of the landowning ladder: owners of 30 to 50 hectares, large enough to mechanize and small enough to avoid much wage labor, and the owners of small estates who opened shops or found jobs and hired their neighbors to work their land.

The *casas* were the cells of social change of Ibieca. In their stories we observe families and individuals making decisions from one day, month, and year to the next about what to produce and how to produce it, each *casa* according to its own timing and imperatives. I have argued that the direction and pace of those decisions was determined by state policies and programs. The *casa* tales show us that a *casa's* family cycle, its place in the agrarian political economy of the village, and individual personalities also shaped its productive decisions, indecisions, and revisions. By focusing on the *casa* as the unit of social reproduction, we may account for both continuity and change in the village economy. We may trace the effects of specific agrarian policies and market conditions and see the village as "a fluid construction that is refashioned daily."[8] When agrarian policies and market conditions change, *casa* decisions shift, and the

---

8. I am grateful to Davydd Greenwood for this formulation.

village economy is altered. In this context social change is a mere side effect, an unintended consequence of the *casas'* adjustments to their environment of opportunities and constraints. Some landowners participated more aggressively than others in the transformation of Ibieca's economy, but all participated unwittingly.

The dissolution of *amo*/laborer and peasant relations of production and the evolution of farming in Ibieca was, of course, more than an economic transformation. The following chapter explores some of the political, social, and cultural ramifications.

⚘ Chapter Six
⚘ Ibieca under the
⚘ Franco Reforms

Ibieca's landscape is broken into small mesas and valleys, and the village itself sits upon the flat expanse of one of the higher mesas. One afternoon Daniel Castillo walked with me to the southern edge of that mesa; as we stood overlooking the gently tortured land spread out to the horizon, he told me, "You can see half the world from here." In 1950, when Daniel was in his prime, Ibieca was very much a world, one that evoked a sense of belonging, that staked a claim of place upon the minds of its people. The landscape before the eyes of Daniel's grandchildren in 1975, or even before those of his son, Mariano, was not a whole world, not even half a world. It had shrunk and lost meaning. It was merely land to be farmed; it yielded profit but not a culture.

In the American literature on village Spain there is some debate about whether emigration and "modernization" have resulted in social atomization and the disintegration of village life. Richard Barrett, among others, argues that such trends eroded community during the 1960s in Benabarre, a town in eastern Huesca, while Stanley Brandes argues that similar trends did not result in the decline of community in Becedes, a village in Avila. Spanish villages have charted remarkably different courses through recent decades, and it is impossible to make specific claims about what is happening in all of them at any one time.[1] Moreover, village life is complex, full of contradictory tendencies and hence open to diverse interpretations. Since many forms of community are alive in Ibieca, I could argue that recent trends have not been so destructive. How-

---

1. For the range of variation, in addition to Barrett, *Benabarre*; and Brandes, *Migration, Kinship, and Community*, see: Aceves and Douglass, *Changing Faces*; Douglass, *Echalar and Murelaga*; Fraser, *Tajos*; Gilmore, *People of the Plain*; Hansen, *Rural Catalonia*; Kenny, *Spanish Tapestry*; Lisón-Tolosana, *Belmonte*; and Pérez-Díaz, *Pueblos y clases*.

ever, there can be little question that the overall direction of rural Spanish society is toward what might be called social atomization and the disintegration of village life.

The world of Daniel still haunted Ibieca while I was there in the 1970s, enchanting us with its sense of wholeness, belonging, and meaning. That sense of place emanated from the dense material connections, the deep social roots, and the multidimensional interdependencies among individuals, families, land, animals, and the elements that characterized the agricultural organization of Daniel's world. It lingered in the village, but it will not be reproduced in the social world coalescing around Daniel's grandchildren and their peers. That "sense" was lost with the agrarian reformation wrought by Mariano Castillo and his generation. In this chapter I shall spell out how it was lost by describing the unmaking of its experiential bases within *casas* and within the village as a whole.

The Reorganization of the Casa

The *casa* was the eye of the storm of agrarian reorganization in the sense that village families navigated in relation to the continuity of their *casas*. The *casa* was their continuous unit of reference, but it did not emerge unchanged. As village families remade their methods and relations of production, they also remade social and political relations within and between *casas*. The ramifications were countless, and my intent here is only to highlight those which led to the demise of Ibieca as an experiential whole, a moral universe. Within the *casa* the key processes of decay were the draining away of authority from parents and of prestige from heirs, the *casa's* dissolution as an ecological whole, and the urbanization of family rites.

We have seen that, before the Civil War, Julia Javones was vilified for abandoning her husband's inheritance and their obligations to his parents, whereas Julia's sons, Angela Iglesias's son, and other heirs have done likewise in more recent years without incurring social disapprobation. Angela was deeply upset by Ismael's decision to move to Huesca with his wife in 1965, but she did not disinherit him, and by 1975 she even spoke of the decision as if it made sense.

Tomás Coronas was furious at his son for deciding to move to Huesca with his bride and to build his own house in Ibieca for weekend visits, but, short of voicing his feelings, he made no effort to stop Joaquín, and other villagers took his plans in stride.

These examples indicate the slow demise of the stem family as a household form and as a moral universe. Between 1950 and 1970 the proportion of stem-family *casas, casas* in which a married couple and retired parents lived together, dropped from one-third to one-fifth. While the above examples also describe the decline of power and authority of parents specifically over heirs, the pattern of decline was broader still. Children were freeing themselves from parental authority in general—as at Mariano Castillo's feast-day meal, when the younger generation of siblings and cousins stunned their parents with their liberal moral code and lax work ethic. The decline of parental authority was perhaps most eloquently registered in the change in usage of the formal forms of "you" between parents and children. All parents called their children *tu*, the informal term. Children who were raised before the 1960s called their parents *usted*, the formal form. Children raised since 1960 called their parents *tu*. The change from an unreciprocal usage to a reciprocal one reflected a significant contraction in the subjectively experienced authority differential in the parent-child relationship.

Courting patterns also registered the decline of parental control. To be on speaking terms was no longer a sign of engagement between a young woman and man; young people interacted in various ways daily, and dances and mixed excursions to the city were frequent. When Sara Segarra and Mariano Castillo were young, they went to feast-day dances in surrounding villages only when invited by resident kin or close friends. They were distressed by the fact that their son and his friends drove to feast-day dances every weekend during the summer months—but they did not stop him. Consonant with this greater contact and freedom of movement, young women and men have more personal control over whom they will marry. In the past parental control had been largely indirect—there were few literally arranged marriages—and structured by the parents' control over their children's social relations. Still, it had been sufficient to enable parents to extend and reinforce their own networks through children's marriages. By the 1970s, in contrast, marriage was in the hands of the children, and how it affected their parents' social networks was incidental.

The other dramatic change in the social relations of the *casa* involved the reversal of status between heirs and non-heirs. No matter how modest the *casa*, its heir had been the high-ranking, most fortunate, sibling. The heir and his or her spouse were economically favored; they were at the center of a web of kin and affines; and theirs was an honorable and morally superior occupation. By 1970 the settlements awarded to non-heirs were substantial in many small as well as large landholding families. Some parents, or the heir, bought city apartments for non-heirs when they married; others paid the settlement in the form of a college education. The nonheir's future seemed open and the heir's foreshortened; the heir had lost special status and was acquiring an aura of being the unfortunate, disadvantaged, socially inferior sibling.

During the 1950s and 1960s neither the agrarian reform nor these familial changes compromised the custom of impartible inheritance in Ibieca, and hence the landholding pattern and the *casa* as a unit of house, land, and family remained relatively stable. While I was there I detected no shift away from impartible inheritance, but it was clear the inheritance system was in crisis. Some *casa* owners had no heirs in mind. Some, like Tomás Coronas, were locked in a losing battle over the terms of the inheritance—either Tomás gave in to Joaquín, or he lost his heir. Others relinquished control over their estates completely and voluntarily. Gregorio Agustín's mother died without a will, so her *casa* was divided evenly among her children. Gregorio bought his siblings' shares and titled the whole *casa* in his unmarried son's name. In doing so, Gregorio forfeited customary authority over Pascual and his legal rights to the *casa*'s income and residence in order to maximize his son's interest in its survival.

The old inheritance and family systems of Ibieca had generated enduring estates and episodic stem families with clear hierarchies of parents over children and heirs over non-heirs. The *casa* and its heirs were the nexus of a kinship web that was spun anew in each generation, as siblings married into neighboring *casas* or moved to cities near and far. The *casa*, as a perpetual homestead, gave roots to kin; wherever one lived, one *pertenicido a* (belonged to) Ibieca.

Although the custom of passing the *casa* on to a single heir persisted through the 1970s, everything else was shifting and the *casa*'s role in grounding a world of kin was dissolving. Even if an heir married, lived with his or her parents in the patrimonial home, and actively worked the land, the social meaning of the *casa* was not the same. Heirs gained power and authority relative to their parents at the same time that they lost prestige alongside their migrant siblings. Marriage was less a means of reproducing the *casa* and its social relations than of establishing one's own nuclear world. Although relations with natal kin continued to be emotionally and socially strong for life, adulthood was becoming more a matter of escaping parental authority than of accepting it. *Casas* still attracted kin and affines for holidays, weekends, and summers, but among the younger generation resident heirs had ceased to center the webs of kinship and affinity. Ibieca was not, in the same sense, where migrant siblings *belonged*; it was where they got away from the city and felt "at home." The *casa* as a social institution, if not as an entity of property and persons, was unmade during the agrarian reorganization of Ibieca, and its unmaking pulled the linchpin out of the kinship system.

At the same time, the *casa* was dissolved as an ecological whole. Full mechanization at once transformed the connection between men and the land and between fathers and sons. One of the sources of a father's authority in a preindustrial *casa* was his intimate knowledge of its fields, gardens, orchards, and vineyards, of the terrain of Ibieca generally, of the weather and the wind. That intimacy with the earth and that dependence of the son on his father were rendered obsolete as tractors and combines displaced mules, plows, reapers, and threshers, as cereals replaced vineyards and orchards. A farmer's intimate knowledge nowadays concerns machinery, agricultural credit, fertilizers, state agrarian subsidies, and crop insurance; his relationship to the land and the elements is more instrumental, even mechanical.

With the decline in intimacy between family and land there came a break in the integrity of the *casa* as productive whole. The primary purpose of daily activity in most *casas* before 1950 was to grow, harvest, slaughter, and process food for the table; meals were almost wholly composed of homegrown foods. By 1975 the primary purpose of daily work for those families still active in agriculture

Village and city kin visit outside Casa Sánchez

was to raise food for market, and most of the makings of any meal were purchased from one of the village's two grocery stores. Most of the material cycles of which village families used to be a part encircled them within village boundaries, rendering a palpable moral whole. Every minute decision to increase market involvement broke links in those local cycles, and by 1975 Ibieca and its *casas* were just way stations in world economic cycles.

When I first arrived in Ibieca, Casa Castillo, where I boarded, still raised chickens and hens. The chickens were kept for special occasions—not for major feast days (when lambs were slaughtered), but for minor feast days and visits from siblings' families. The chickens lived in the stable area near the kitchen, picking their fare out of scraps and feed cast their way after every family meal. Sara Segarra would select a plump chicken in the morning, bring it into the kitchen, cut its throat over the sink, pluck it, wash it, cut it up, and roast it for the midday meal.

We all agreed that those chickens tasted better than the granja *fowl. When I wondered why, I was told that* granja *chickens were fed chemicals to make them grow faster and fatter and that they were never as fresh; preservatives and refrigeration robbed them of flavor, too. Mariano and Sara told me similar tales about* granja *pork and eggs, store-bought wine, olive oil, and milk. Merchants put chemicals into them, and powders, and they water them down. Homegrown and homemade food is fresher and pure—that's why it tastes better.*

The villagers of Ibieca were not generally nostalgic about what they were losing materially for all the changes in recent decades. No one under sixty missed their plows and mules or pondered what they had lost by mechanizing agricultural work. No one eulogized the kitchen hearth and disparaged the butane stove. They did not prefer the wooden board above the manure pile over their flush toilets, or their rustic handmade tables, chairs, and chests over their veneered and lacquered furniture. I do not know why home-grown food made them so nostalgic.

Whatever tagged food for special feeling, there is a vast difference in the social meaning of homegrown and granja *chickens. The homegrown chicken was hatched from an egg that was laid by a hen that was born and raised in the same barnyard, much as chickens and hens have been born and raised there for centuries. It was fed on scraps from a table around which sat a family that descended from generations of families who lived in the same house and nearby houses. The scraps and feed were the ultimate products of crops and livestock raised by the family for its own table. The chicken, in short, was a part of a material and social whole that composed a* casa. *Eating it was an experience of that whole and of its continuity. The social meaning of a homegrown chicken was as rich as its flavor.*

The granja *chicken, in contrast, was a multinational bird. Chicks were hatched in giant hatcheries owned by regional feed companies that collaborated with multinational feed corporations. They were sold to* granja *owners along with feed and chemicals, raised in cages by the thousands, and sold for slaughter on a schedule set by the feed company's computerized assessment of national and international market conditions. The* granja *chicken did not represent any meaningful whole; eating it was an experience of fragmenta-*

tion, of the casa *as dependent and trivial, a tiny speck in world economic cycles utterly beyond the vision of villagers.*

The dispersal of most major family life-cycle events and rituals also diminished the experience of the *casa* as a whole. There have been no weddings or births in Ibieca since the late 1950s; young people have married in city churches instead, and their children are now born in city hospitals. During the 1960s and 1970s families also increasingly took their ill and elderly to hospitals as they neared death. Funerals and burials were the only major life-cycle links left unbroken, and on those occasions villagers often re-marked on the absence of other family-making rites from the vil-lage. They noted that funerals had come to signify the end of the village as well as of individual lives.

The removal of dying and death from Ibieca has a special signifi-cance in the disintegration of the *casa* and the village, contributing both to the emaciation of villagers' sense of the past and to the rise of consumerism. Villagers kept their past alive through storytelling, and the storyteller "borrowed his authority from death." In Walter Benjamin's words, "Not only a man's knowledge or wisdom, but above all his real life—and this is the stuff that stories are made of—first assumes transmissible form at the moment of his death. Just as a sequence of images is set in motion inside a man as his life comes to an end—unfolding the views of himself under which he has en-countered himself without being aware of it—suddenly in his ex-pressions and looks the unforgettable emerges and imparts to every-thing that concerned him that authority which even the poorest wretch in dying possesses for the living around him. This is the authority of the storyteller."[2] The removal of death and dying from Ibieca also removed the authority of the storyteller, of the story of a life, triggered by death, and hence of the past as a presence in the village.

Most urban observers write as if the growth of consumerism were natural, assuming that villagers wanted consumer goods as soon as they were exposed to them, that bourgeois values were either conta-gious or genetic. In *Pig Earth* John Berger reminds us that peasants

2. Benjamin, *Illuminations*, p. 94.

are by their social nature conservationists, and that their resistance to consumption had to be actively broken down.[3] Breaking it down, according to Berger, involved undermining the authority of the past on the one hand and reorienting persons toward future transformations of self on the other hand. In preconsumer capitalist cultures, Death—the personification of death—was "the surrogate for a generalized sense of uncertainty and menace in the face of the future."[4] Removing death, hence Death, from the village at once liberated the face of the future from its pall and compromised the authority of the past. Thus it was one of the social processes that helped make Ibieca safer for consumerism, for the ceaseless consumption of new images of one's self.

All of the social processes discussed so far contributed to the gradually growing availability of *casas* for market sale. Until the early nineteenth century most rural property was absolutely beyond the pale of the market in Spain due to privileges of entailment and mortmain. The grip of impartible inheritance of rural property in Ibieca was looser but still fairly tight. Land was sold and *casas* dismantled only as a consequence of extreme debt or fantastic misfortune. As *casas* lose their moral, social, and material unity, the idea of working oneself to the bone for a *casa*'s survival loses its capacity to give life meaning, and the idea of selling *casas* loses its stigma. To sell or not to sell a *casa* becomes a practical and a sentimental matter. If selling becomes more common, the market will squeeze still more of the sense of place out of Ibieca.

New Lines of Sociability, Faith, and Politics

We have seen that the village, as well as the *casa*, has withered as a material and productive whole in recent decades; the dilution of kin ties has likewise weakened the village and its families. The capitalist agrarian reform transformed strong social relations of production among *amo*, laborer, and peasant families into weaker rental and wage-work arrangements. A few collective productive ar-

3. Berger, *Pig Earth*, p. 210.
4. Ibid., p. 203.

rangements among *casas*, such as the group combine and the village sheep flock, survived the 1970s, but the financial squeeze was threatening them, too. As a result of the reorganization of productive relations and of emigration, kinship and marriage will not bind the next generation of villagers to each other as those relations bound their parents into a strong affective community.

Other social links connecting *casas* and making the village an experiential whole have been or are being broken by the agrarian reform and other transformative processes. Villagers experienced themselves as connected in public spaces, in church, and in politics, as well as through productive and kin relations. In examining the evolution of those connections in recent decades, we may see at least two subpatterns in the overall scheme: men were disconnected more, or sooner, than women; and at the same time youths did not reproduce old connections that made *casas* and the village whole, they made new connections that linked them as much to the city, the region, and the nation as to Ibieca.

The village fountain, once the site of continuous and diverse social and productive interactions, was rarely crowded and often deserted by the late 1970s. When running water was installed, villagers all but stopped fetching water from the fountain. Young men and women had many other places to linger and mingle, to see and be seen by each other. The mules, asses, oxen, and horses were gone, and only the herds of Juan Solano and Luis Segarra clambered down for water each day at dawn and dusk. As families bought washing machines, women stopped lining the washbasin, kneeling to wash clothes and gossip. Even irrigation was beginning to fall off as an activity that gathered villagers at the fountain, as families gave up gardening. Likewise, the school was much less a link among village families. Forty children used to attend on weekdays for all their schooling; by 1975 only a half-dozen were attending, and these only for their early years. Older children were bussed to Barbastro and Huesca schools, and even their numbers had been cut drastically by families' emigrating and having fewer children. The village bar, on the other hand, was becoming the hot spot of daily village life. When the elderly couple that ran it for decades retired, village youths and the priest formed a cooperative to renovate and operate it. Once the lair of men who drank, smoked cigars, and played cards, under its youthful cooperative management the bar was filled every night with villagers of both sexes and all ages.

So village life was losing its special character and becoming more like city life. Religious practice and the priest registered similar tendencies. The confraternity of village men which functioned as a kind of burial society never recovered after the Civil War. The custom of tapping four men in rotation to carry a neighbor's coffin to the cemetery survived, but they were released from gravedigging when the municipal government began hiring a trencher. Village women have been tapped in rotation, too, as *madalesas*, to carry out a variety of religious duties. By 1975 the *madalesas* had lost all their functions except cleaning the church and filling it with fresh flowers on summer Sundays. Regular church services and activities, which had once appealed to villagers to gather two or three times a day, were reduced to daily mass. In the 1970s most villagers still attended Sunday mass, but only four women, Angela Iglesias and the three elderly women from Casas Solano and Blanco, attended weekday mass regularly.

Several minor processions suspended during the Civil War were never held again. During the 1940s villagers went on a few processions with other central Somontano villages to pray to Santa María de Liesa for rain, but those processions stopped during the late 1950s. When I asked villagers why they stopped going on such processions, some shrugged their shoulders, and some proposed that rainfall was not the problem it used to be (because tractor plowing released more moisture into the soil). The only processions carried out in Ibieca in the 1970s were those in which the image of the Virgin of Foces was carried from the village church to the chapel in the fields each fall and back again each spring. Although the devotion of some villagers to the Virgin of Foces remained strong, her role as a symbol and protector of the village, its fields and its people, was weaker.

Village priests were the instigators of many of the changes in religious practice. The actions and attitudes of Ibieca's priest, Manuel Bueno, during the 1970s indicated the scale of change since 1950, when, according to Angela Iglesias, priests were still lordly. Manuel wore grey slacks and a knit shirt, not a black cassock. Far from manifesting the aloofness of his predecessors, he interacted most

*The Lacasa brothers carrying the Virgin of Foces in the
yearly procession*

Fields and Foces (right), the Virgin's winter dominion

easily with young people, went with them to dances regularly, and, although he did not dance, joked and laughed with them, as Angela put it, "as if he were no different." Manuel did not instruct village children in religion, though he helped them with schoolwork and joined young men and women to organize the bar, feast-day games, and other social events. According to Angela, Manuel performed a "fleeced mass"—just the bare essentials. He eliminated daily confession early in his tenure, a loss which deeply disturbed some village women. Later he withdrew even from the mandatory Easter confession of the village, instead asking a priest from another village to exchange parishes with him so that he did not have to confess his own parish. Manuel did not want to know the sins of Ibieca.

During his stay in Ibieca, Manuel came to respect the faith and the rituals of villagers, but when he first arrived he referred to them as superstitions and told me he would rather hold a weekly concert in the church than a Sunday mass. In the course of a conversation in which Manuel had hoped to learn from me how an American (that is, a technocrat) could believe in God, he told me he was a humanist and believed God was in the Brotherhood of Man. In another conversation, late in the 1970s, we talked about the role of the priest in

Manuel Bueno, the village priest

village social life. Manuel said that priests had once had a role in village family life; they had formulas to solve family problems, ideas about how to behave, and faith to sustain people in need of guidance and support. The problems had not changed so much as the entire framework of family life had altered; the old formulas did not work anymore, and the Church had not evolved new ones. Manuel said that some priests continued to offer old formulas, but he and his friends did not. They did not claim to know how to solve people's personal and family problems, and many parishioners had stopped coming to them with their dilemmas.

The priest in Ibieca once united the village in sacred ceremonies and inculcated beliefs that shored up family and village hierarchies—of parents over children, of men over women, and of *amos* over all. Manuel Bueno completed the shift away from service to those hierarchies. Priests were evolving a variety of new roles in the countryside, and Manuel found himself most comfortable working with village youth in their pursuit of secular knowledge and in their collective pursuits of leisure. He was aware of the religious feeling of some of his elder parishioners, and he tended to them by performing basic rites. But that religious feeling was intrinsic to the old world of Ibieca, and Manuel could scarcely understand where it came from and could not contribute to reproducing it. He was a priest of the new world, not the old.[5]

I have described two kinds of politics in old Ibieca. One kind emerged from, was an aspect of, productive relations and defined persons as either equal or unequal and specified the terms of solidarity or hierarchy. The other kind of politics involved organized activity aimed at gaining access to or manipulating government resources. In old Ibieca the politics of productive relations organized—even absorbed—formal politics; hence the agrarian reform, combined with dictatorial political reforms, radically altered the village as a political organism. These politics were largely the politics of men. Before discussing their transfiguration I shall examine gossip, which was largely the politics of women. I could not recover this political form in my excavation of Ibieca's past, so I present it here in some detail.

In a face-to-face society, knowledge of others exists on two levels: that which is public and that which is not. Gossip, by definition, circulates private knowledge, knowledge that a person does not want others to have and that others generally prevent a person from knowing they have about him or her. In Ibieca prime topics for gossip were inheritance battles, conflicts between family members and neighbors, illicit sexual liaisons and premarital pregnancies, bizarre behavior and personality traits, shady deals, and dishonorable deeds. Gossip often appeared to be the simple reporting of conversations and events from scenes participated in, observed, or heard about by

5. See Christian, *Person and God,* for a full discussion of the contemporary transformation of religious life in a Spanish valley.

the reporter, as if women were quite neutrally keeping each other posted on village lives.

Gossip was a system for circulating real information, but that was never all that was circulated. Although overt criticism was rare, covert evaluation was constant. An indirect evaluation was built into the report or failure to report a conversation, a deed, or an event. As the report was given, editing continued, with the speaker highlighting and omitting portions so that further evaluation was written between the lines, even when it was not stated in so many words.

Sometimes gossip seemed to start idly, in response to a question; other times it was clearer that a woman actively intended to communicate some information or an opinion. Vital information, about death or serious illness, passed around the village as fast as women could open their windows and call across to their neighbors. More confidential words did not move so fast or freely, encountering resistance and moving in smaller circles. Words spread, stumbled, died, doubled back, were reborn and transformed. Some made things better; some made things worse; some made no difference at all. The overall movement and effect of the messages seemed random and beyond any individual control or design. But at each link, movement and effect were not random or accidental. A woman usually had her reasons for saying the things she said.

Men and women appeared to be working in opposite directions in the politics of private life. Men controlled the economic and political affairs in and between *casas*; for their part, in secrecy lay power and defense, in privacy reposed peace and order. If it was the role of men to build and maintain the figurative fences between *casas*, it was the role of women to climb those fences from time to time. Many women pursued the role with vigor, but also with considerable care. Women probed privacies; they did not invade them. They were not telling and gleaning family secrets; they were piecing together essential interpretations of village lives according to their definition of relevance. They were, quite literally, integrating the village. Their gossip created village society daily.

Women's gossip in Ibieca, as in other male-dominant societies, had a reputation for disrupting the social order. Yet, as I observed it, gossip contributed to reproducing the social order; indeed, it was constitutive of order within and between families. Women in their gossip were operating with their family interest in mind. They were operating not outside the value system, but within it, as it shaped both what they said and what they heard. Gossip had a bad name in Ibieca because, in gossiping, women were behaving politically; gossip gave women power, and power was not the cultural prerogative of women. Women's words were the stuff reputations were made of, and in small communities reputations are powerful because they help determine one's actual relations and scope of action. Power was man's prerogative in Ibieca, and gossip challenged men's control over the social order. Even though it reproduced that order, gossip was the politics of the officially powerless and was therefore imbued with connotations of wickedness and wrongdoing.

The constant cultural campaign against women's gossip found allies in the agrarian reform and other processes transforming Ibieca. Women had never gathered just to gossip; rather, gossip occurred around the edges of other interactions among women, so that as those interactions were suspended gossip waned, too. The village washbasin had a legendary reputation for malicious gossip, and perhaps it was valid in a time when the village was more crowded and poorer, when tensions were higher and tempers shorter. In the late 1970s, however, gatherings at the basin were quite benign and thinning out as more families bought washing machines. Breadbaking circles, which had once joined women weekly, were broken in the early 1950s when the Lacasas opened their bakery. Sewing and knitting circles that gathered around doorstoops in the late afternoon were thinning, too, as purchased garments displaced homemade clothes. The mechanization and commercialization of homemaking have all but eliminated gossip sites, and women were left with errands or chance meetings during which to exchange their views—while borrowing something from a neighbor, or on the way to the bakery, the grocery store, or the garden. As women's political discourse withered, one more way in which the village was rendered whole dwindled with it.

Formal politics in old Ibieca were structured by the organization of the state and by productive relations. Before Franco, governmental policies and actions sometimes suspended political competition, sometimes favored *caciques* and their cliques, and sometimes

Chatting in the street while doing errands

opened the political arena to other political parties and unions. Under Franco, state reforms first suspended all political competition, then unmade the agrarian basis of village politics, then renovated the structure of formal politics. Before the Civil War, control of labor, and hence of votes, translated into political power for *amos*; both *amo*/laborer and peasant production generated hierarchical and egalitarian connections among *casas* more generally and rendered Ibieca a political community. In contrast, connections among *casas* based on farming arrangements were just that: they did not render Ibieca a political community. The agrarian reforms themselves dissolved the political presence of the peasantry. *Amos* were debased socially as they lost their control over labor, and political reforms attacked the governmental basis of caciqual power more directly.

Before reviewing the political reforms, we must first note the degree of sheer political repression under Franco, a circumstance that goes a long way toward explaining why villages displayed little challenge or resistance to the capitalist agrarian reform.

A dictatorship by definition extinguishes popular politics. Citizens are prohibited from acting collectively to increase their access to or control over the state apparatus, and only state-organized political activity is permitted. Under Franco, political organizations on both the left and the right were decimated during the Civil War and by systematic repression thereafter. No leftists were executed by Franco's army in Ibieca, but several families that had been most politically active during the war moved to Barcelona or into exile in France. All mobilization against policies was prohibited, and the government operated the only legal trade unions and the only political party, the Movimiento (formerly called Falange). Government permission was required for a group of twenty or more persons to meet for any reason. Elections were suspended or tightly controlled. Finally, the Franco regime owned or effectively managed and censored all means of communication and education. A phrase often uttered to describe the politics of life under Franco was, "If it isn't prohibited, it's compulsory."

In the Somontano the Civil Guard, or rural police force, patrolled villages, although the Movimiento was probably more effective than the Guard in preventing subversive activity. Movimiento liaisons in the Somontano gathered information about everyone from village allies and consulted those allies regarding the appointment and election of village officials. Elections of village councillors were eventually reinstituted; candidates were selected by the provincial Minister of the Interior, and the mayor was appointed on the basis of advice from Movimiento liaisons. Officially everyone in Ibieca belonged to the Movimiento or to some section of it, but the party had no effective existence apart from membership cards and lists, and surveillance. Few villagers bothered with voting, and some were only vaguely aware that elections occurred.

Before Primo de Rivera's regime in the 1920s, elections had been a forum for competition among personalistic factions dominated by village *amos*, all of whom wanted privileged access to government resources. During the Second Republic moderate and left-wing parties dominated by small landowners and craftsmen joined the competition. By eliminating that forum, Franco suspended caciqual politics as well as popular mobilization in Ibieca. The fact that provincial appointees of the central government in turn appointed mayors reflected its authority and cut further into the power of village *caciques*. However, in Ibieca the head or close relative of the head of one of the caciqual houses was appointed mayor for twenty-seven of the thirty-seven years of Franco's rule. For nineteen of those years, the head of Casa Solano was mayor. Although the mayor's principal mandate was to represent village needs to provincial officials and to obtain benefits for the village, many mayors concentrated on using the office to line their own pockets—for example, by cultivating wheat on municipal land without paying rent. At least through the 1960s, Franco's government suspended caciqual politics but not *caciques*, who retained considerable power in the structures of municipal government.

Beginning effectively in the 1960s, the Franco regime transformed village government and the nature of political resources in the countryside. New resources were funneled into the village through the village secretary's office, rather than through the mayor. The two officials were often in cahoots and could still dip into the spoils to some extent, but pension payments, for example, were determined in Madrid and were immune to pilfering. The social security system represented an important centralization and bureaucratization of state power, and it compromised *caciques* by bypassing the mayors' office and by making poor villagers still less dependent on *amos* for wage work. In the late 1960s there was a concerted centralization effort in the form of a campaign to fuse village governments in the Somontano into larger and presumably more efficient administrative units. The state offered incentives, from fat subsidies for various projects, such as paving village streets, to outright payments to village councils in exchange for their governmental autonomy. In effect, the central government was bribing village governments to unite with their neighbors.

By 1973 every village in the central Somontano except Ibieca had relinquished its governmental autonomy. The state, working through the Movimiento, exerted continuous pressure on Mayor Juan Solano to fuse with Angüés. While villagers were basically hostile to the idea of subordinating their government to that of Angüés, it also seemed that Solano had personal interests that he wished to protect from outside scrutiny. Late in 1973 Solano was told that if he did not fuse Ibieca's government, he would be removed as mayor. Misjudging his right to refuse a directive from above, he held out and was removed from office. The appointment of Tomás Lacasa as the new mayor compounded Solano's loss, because Lacasa was not beholden to him.

In somewhat larger terms, the appointment of Lacasa as mayor represented the end of the tacit accord between the Franco regime and village *caciques* in which the suspension of caciqual politics was traded for fairly continuous control of village governments. The Franco regime was transferring control over the mayor's office from the old *amos* to more entrepreneurial villagers. As it turned out, Lacasa's willingness to accommodate the central government by fusing Ibieca with Angüés was never tested. The municipal reform effort petered out shortly after Lacasa's appointment, and Ibieca still had an autonomous government in 1980.

In 1979, in the first mayoral election after Franco's death in 1975, Juan Solano was elected mayor. His victory reflected his lingering caciqual power but not the reemergence of *caciquismo*, as we can see by scrutinizing the election and his subsequent comportment in office. Solano did not win the election on the basis of his control over votes, or even on the basis of his votes. Rather, he was chosen from those elected to the village council. Five men ran for the five seats, so all were "elected." Only one candidate received fewer votes than Solano, Ramón Lacasa, who had not lived full-time in Ibieca for several years. The three candidates who received more votes were Martín Miranda and Pascual Agustín, both small landowners in their twenties, and Ricardo Sánchez, a large landowner in his forties. Each in turn was invited to become the mayor of Ibieca; each accepted his council seat but refused the mayor's office. Pascual told me he refused because he feared he would be in a position of having to tolerate Solano's long-standing venality or to expose it and suffer the consequences of the ensuing battle. Pascual's refusal at once reflected Solano's residual power and the unwillingness of others to submit to it. Juan Solano was eventually offered and accepted the post; and thus he became mayor more by default than by election.

Juan Solano had lost the basis of his social power in the village. He had no way of imposing his will on villagers, and during his first year as mayor the village council came to define its task as making Solano more accountable, at least in so far as he represented the village in Huesca. In 1970, when I asked him what he did as mayor of Ibieca, Solano told me, "Nothing," but in 1979 he was cultivating more of a public image. Since he was slow to act on his own initiative in village interests, the council defined those interests for him and instructed him to act. He had bungled an effort to secure funds for a village grain scale—a project he did not himself endorse—and the younger council members were trying to convince him to support the referendum on forming an Aragonese regional goverment. Younger men and women seemed far better able to garner resources for the village from the provincial government through informal channels than the mayor could through both formal and informal channels. It was clear, however, that some sort of table had turned in Ibieca's history. Once the mayor was the *amo*'s agent; now the *amo* was the villagers' agent. Some even spoke of Solano with sympathy, as if he were an emperor who had lost his clothes.

The demise of Franco's regime and the transition to democracy had a tremendous impact on village discourse. Those who had known political activity in Ibieca before Franco seized power were old, retiring, and generally cynical. Everyone under fifty had matured in a politically aseptic world, and while Franco was alive most described themselves as apolitical and apathetic. What I saw when I returned in 1976, about eight months after Franco's death, demonstrated how much the demobilization had depended on the promise of state repression. Villagers once watched their words politically, weighed the consequences before speaking, and censored themselves about the government and politicians. When Franco died, villagers began to speak directly and to develop political opinions, not only about the government and politicians but also about political parties (still illegal at the time) and what kind of democracy they wanted. Almost overnight, the double thinking disappeared. The change was at once subtle and immense, as if a great invisible weight were quietly slipping from their minds.

Spain in the late 1970s was a riot of new political parties, agrarian organizations, platforms, programs, and voices. With the old political back of the countryside broken by the demise of the peasantry and *caciquismo*, how would villagers behave in the opening political arena? Some declared their sympathies with particular parties or unions, but no one in Ibieca organized a local chapter or was active in a chapter elsewhere. When the government called for candidates for village councils in 1979, no one in Ibieca or in many surrounding villages presented himself to run. Ramón Lacasa, who lived in Huesca but was still a legal resident of Ibieca and a member of the governing party, the Union of the Democratic Center (UCD), called a meeting and convinced four men to run with him on the UCD slate. Ramón also brought the UCD candidate for the national senate to Ibieca; the questions asked by some of the older men revealed that they still expected politicians to act as patrons in exchange for their votes. Nicolás Cabrero told me that he did not vote for the UCD candidate because, when Nicolás asked him if he would channel money to Ibieca to pave its roads, the candidate avoided answering the question. The new political etiquette did not sanction open horse-trading for votes, but Nicolás still did and concluded the candidate was not a good politician, so did not vote for him.

Indications were that, for the time being, internally generated political action in villages like Ibieca would focus on single issues if it occurred at all. In 1975 villages in the southeastern part of the province, along the Cinca River, organized a sixty-mile march to Huesca to protest construction of a nuclear reactor that would heat up the river, change the weather, and threaten agriculture in the area. A cavalcade of tractors, trucks, and cars carried 4,000 villagers to Huesca to demonstrate in city streets. In several high mountain valleys, villagers organized mass actions to block the construction of dams that would inundate their villages. During the first five years of democracy no such issue roused the villagers of Ibieca to collective protest. As for party politics, villagers were not totally disinterested, but politics seemed removed from their lives, somehow alien. The end of the dictatorship had dramatically changed political discourse in the village, but it had not altered political behavior very much. Villagers elected village councillors and, indirectly, their mayor, but otherwise politics in Ibieca still consisted of village officials and villagers in general working toward a vague consensus about a village need and village officials trying to fill that need by securing support from the provincial goverment in Huesca.

There was one striking difference: young men and women were becoming a political force, crucial both in achieving consensus and in securing resources. They were also building some bridges toward a different political future. In January, 1976, five young single women whose political awareness outstripped that of their male peers organized a series of cultural events, Jornadas Culturales, for Ibieca. They wanted to bring to the village some of the ideas and personalities that were animating others in the province. A nationally known provincial historian, Antonio Durán, spoke about Somontano social history; Aurelio Biarge, a lawyer and historian who was emerging as one of the province's new politicans, spoke about problems of underdevelopment; a folksinger, José Antonio Labordeta, sang songs that combined traditional tunes and lyrics of regional protest. For three afternoons the village schoolhouse was packed with people of all ages from Ibieca and neighboring villages. The cultural events were so successful that the young women organized them again the following year. Younger villagers, at least, seemed to be developing a political culture—reclaiming the old one to some extent, but mainly creating a new one. They were very much concerned about Ibieca and its needs, but they were also constructing a regional political consciousness, an Aragonese identity that bridged city and countryside. Their parents had city ties, but they experienced them mainly as extensions of village life. In contrast, young people in Ibieca were not so centered in the village; they traveled easily and often to the city, and their primary political communities were the region and the nation, not Ibieca.

The cultural gap between children and parents in Ibieca is wide, much wider than the one between parents and grandparents. The parents built a new economic and social order within the material and moral universe of the grandparents. Their worlds are intermeshed, but the union cannot continue to reproduce itself. The parents' renovations have already gone a long way toward diluting the mixture of autonomy and connection, authority and equality, nature and culture, birth and death that once yielded the *casas* and Ibieca, the community of *casas*. Many children hope to keep both their *casas* and the community alive, but they will do so on terms very different from those of their parents. Whether they can succeed, and on what terms, remains to be seen. Moreover, the future is not yet in their hands.

It is a precarious historical moment for agriculture in Ibieca and the Somontano. Apart from the fact that many *casas* do not have heirs, the economic viability of agriculture for another generation is not assured. In this context, several proposals to form a capitalist agrarian cooperative have surfaced in recent years. They hold out the possibility of the village assuming some collective control over its future—a prospect that many greet with mixed feelings, as the next chapter demonstrates. In discussing the debate over whether to form an agrarian cooperative, we may recognize the constraints, old and new, structural and idiosyncratic, on community action. We may also appreciate villagers' ongoing capacity to act collectively and the degree to which the village future is open ended.

✸ Chapter Seven
✸ The Agrarian
✸ Cooperative Debates

When Andrés Castro and Juan Blanco proposed a cooperative in the mid-1960s, they called in provincial agents from the National Service of Plot Concentration. The agents explained the advantages of both concentrating their landholdings and setting up a complete production cooperative. All land work would be done with cooperatively owned machinery, with the profits from crop and livestock sales distributed according to the holdings of each cooperative member. The principal advantage would come from cutting the costs of production. Members would need fewer machines and fewer workers; they could obtain discounts on fertilizers and other productive goods by buying them in bulk; they would be eligible for subsidies and low-interest government loans to develop the enterprise.

The second proposal, a more modest one, was made in the late 1970s by Fernando Badía and Tomás Lacasa. They called in Pascual Laguna, the Agricultural Extension Agent in Angüés, to discuss the virtues of a modern sheep cooperative. They proposed establishing a co-op that would begin on a small scale and grow steadily. Sheep would be stabled in one large facility each night, and their feed would be grown on land rented from village houses. Members would own shares rather than certain sheep, and benefits would be distributed according to shares. With modern organization, the sheep would produce more lambs, the cost of feed and labor would be lowered, and villagers would be relieved of the burden of stabling their own sheep each night. Again, they would be eligible for subsidies and low-interest government loans.

The proposals were presented at public meetings which most village men attended. In each instance there were a couple of hours of animated questioning, criticism, and discussion, and the meetings dissipated before any decisions were reached. More discussion among pairs and small groups of men occurred during the following weeks; then it, too, dissipated, and the proposals were gradually dropped. Dropped, but not forgotten by many village men, who thought that cooperative organization made sense and would benefit them all. They recognized that a cooperative would increase productivity and therefore incomes; that it would make them independent of, yet benefit, their heirs; and that the state conferred real advantages on cooperative organization. Nevertheless, they let the opportunity pass not once, but twice. Why? And why did other men resist still more, making light of the benefits of cooperative organization? I asked a dozen men these questions. Their answers raise an old specter in scholarly debates about peasants and poverty, one variously labeled amoral familism, the culture of poverty, peasant individualism, and familial particularism. The common notion is that villagers are prevented from acting collectively on their own behalf by their values, their culture. I will argue that such an interpretation misconstrues the men's discourse on the cooperative proposals. However, the usual counterappeal to political economic obstacles is not completely compelling, either. How can we understand the passive resistance of village men to the two cooperative proposals in a way that does not render them mere victims of values and circumstances beyond their control?

Many men used the same phrase to describe their response to the cooperative proposals that they used to describe their response to anarchist collectivization: "We are not prepared" (*no somos preparados*). Juan García elaborated by saying that his neighbors thought their fields were the best ones and did not want to exchange them for anyone else's. They did not know how to work with and for others. They did not know how to risk immediate loss in order to seek future gain. García said villagers were also unable to reach a consensus, to agree on the particulars of a proposal. Someone would always have another way of doing whatever was proposed and would not agree to cooperate unless his way was adopted. García's words were echoed by others: "There is no unity (*unión*) here, we are very divided (*muy separados*). We can't reach a consensus here (*no se ponen en acuerdo aquí*)."

Many men also stressed the divisions among rich and poor. Juan Solano was not in favor of any cooperative effort. He said that he had consolidated his own plots and ran his estate to his satisfaction: "What would I gain from such an arrangement?" According to Tomás Lacasa, the largest landowners were more opposed to the sheep cooperative because they thought they would be providing pasturage and feed to small landowners who had little or none to contribute. In contrast, Lorenzo Lobera and several other small landowners objected to a crop cooperative by saying they would end up working the land of the rich, who would reap the profits. The only crop cooperative proposal that Gregorio Agustín would consent to was one in which all members had equal shares and rented their fields to the cooperative. Rent payments would be unequal, but profits from the crops would accrue to the cooperative and be divided equally among all.

Another common complaint was that the specific proposals for administering a cooperative were unacceptable and that it would be mismanaged. Some claimed that none of the villagers could run such a complex enterprise productively. Others said that they could manage the agricultural end of it well enough, but that they would bungle the bookkeeping, or that there would be fraud. Some specified distrust for Juan Solano, whom they assumed would have the dominant voice in cooperative administration; they said he already misgoverned the village and his own estate.

On the basis of statements such as these, Edward Banfield in *The Moral Basis of a Backward Society* attributed an ethos of "amoral familism" to the inhabitants of a southern Italian town. Banfield argued that the ethos prevented townspeople from acting in any interest but their own family's, and that this locked them into poverty because progress required cooperation and self-sacrifice among families. Amoral familists act as if they are following one rule: "Maximize the material, short-run advantage of the nuclear family; assume that all others will do likewise."[1] Amoral familists will not cooperate with others for the general good, will not take responsibility for the behavior of public officials, will not trust others to act in the common interest, will not initiate or endorse a speculative or a collective action and will not trust anyone who does.

The discourse of village men about the cooperative proposals sets

---

1. Banfield, *Backward Society*, p. 85.

them up for such an interpretation. So did the de facto election of Juan Solano as village mayor in 1979, when all three higher vote-getters did not want to be in the position of either fighting or acquiescing to Solano's informal influence. Villagers were abashed that Solano was mayor again, but they had no trouble understanding why the other council members refused the office. Did the amoral familism lead villagers to "elect" Solano and to pass up two proposals to form an agrarian cooperative? Perhaps they were swayed by a relative of amoral familism—peasant individualism or familial particularism. Have "traditional values" in one form or another inserted themselves between villagers and their common good?

We are enveloped by an assumption that capitalistic and liberal-democratic behavior is rational, and thus that noncapitalistic and non–liberal-democratic behavior requires special explanation. Banfield and his intellectual compatriots say that traditional values make a people behave "irrationally." Some authors counter with sensitive interpretations of the values in question so as to remove from them the gloss of irrationality. Thus Davydd Greenwood explains how Basque farmers left their profitable village homesteads for lesser jobs in the city because the city actually offered them more opportunity to fulfill their traditional values of dignity and sociability. Other counter-arguments appeal to the local or larger political economy to account for behavior that rings of irrationality in the Western mind. Sydel Silverman argues that "amoral familism" in southern Italy was an expression of the local agricultural organization and associated social structure. It was rational in that context; if people were to change, the context would have to change first. Jane Schneider and Peter Schneider studied resistance to cooperative formation in western Sicily and argued that the resistance was rational because, given the location of Sicilian agriculture in the world economy, cooperatives would surely fail.[2]

The scholarly debate suggests at least three possible interpretations of the discourse among the men of Ibieca concerning the agrarian cooperative proposals. One would attribute the resistance to villagers' traditional familial, or individualistic, values and the

2. Greenwood, *Unrewarding Wealth*; Silverman, "Agricultural Organization"; Schneider and Schneider, "Economic Dependence."

absence of a morality, or a sense of mutual connection and obligation, that extended beyond the *casa*. Another interpretation would reject the second claim and turn the argument around: traditional agriculture generated an ethos of "moral familism" which was the basis of inter-*casa* cooperation and alliance; it was destroyed by recent capitalist development, and hence villagers rejected the idea of an agrarian cooperative. A third interpretation would propose that the men's discourse reflected an accurate assessment of the risks involved and their reasonable reluctance to gamble their *casas* on a venture that might well fail as a result of shriveling state subsidies and the cost-price squeeze. The interpretations move from casting the villagers as irrational to rational, from the victims of their culture to the victims of their political and economic circumstances.

Alongside the detail of social life in Ibieca over the decades, we can see how these interpretations tend to oversimplify or misconstrue the past, obscure the complexity of the present, and foreclose the future. Certainly both mental and material structures shaped the men's discourse, their decision and indecision—but so did social processes. To culture and political economy I wish to add another perspective in order to interpret Ibieca's cooperative discourse—that of history, as it is lived, not as an impersonal force.

The agrarian cooperative debates and the resistance expressed therein are not simply the residue of values or of an ethos, nor are they some sort of direct reflection of political and economic conditions. They are the outcome of the historical experience and social relationships of villagers, structured by culture and political economy but not determined by them. History—in the sense of individual and collective memories of past actions, interactions, and inactions—haunts the village present, giving content to the forms of possibility cast by mental and material structures. Within "history" I also mean to include the personalities of Ibieca, all that variation of character, thought, and action that defies derivation from "structures" or "rules." And "history" includes contingency, an acknowledgment of the extent to which what happened might not have happened, and what did not happen could have happened, and might yet.

Many authors writing about village Spain in the 1960s and the

1970s claimed or implied that villagers changed their agricultural conduct because their values changed, usually as a result of increased urban contact. My reconstruction of the remaking of Ibieca argues forcefully against such an interpretation. Villagers "backed into" remaking their agriculture, society, and politics as they responded to state reforms and market conditions in order to survive as *amos*, peasants, and *casa* heads. Their values did *not* change first; they adapted their agricultural strategies to changing conditions in the world around them, as they always had, but this time in so doing they remade the village and themselves. The suggestion that traditional values blocked villagers from making economically progressive decisions falters here. Not only did villagers make such decisions despite their values, but they also made them *because of* their values.

Those who remade Ibieca are thus an oddly mixed lot: they changed so much in order to stay the same, and they stayed the same by changing so much. Experientially, village men changed as *amos* and peasants in order to stay the same as heads of *casas*. The *casa* as a social and material entity was nevertheless unmade, as was the social identity of *casa* head. But the main ingredients of a *casa*—family, land, house—were still assembled, and even weekend farmers sustained a sense of control of the process of agricultural production. Village men had unwittingly transformed their *casas* and themselves as they responded to the capitalist agrarian reforms, and the agrarian cooperative proposals confronted them directly with the final coup. They would have to relinquish the productive integrity of the *casa* completely. Unlike the other transformations, this one was recognizable before the fact. They could feel and measure how much they would lose by joining a cooperative.

Giving up the *casa* meant different things to men who had been peasants and those who had been *amos*, to those who rented their tractor time to others and to those who hired it. Juan Solano and Luis Segarra, the two large landowners whose *casas* and personalities still echoed most of *amo* understandings, were most uninterested in joining their neighbors in an agrarian cooperative. The other large landowners were more interested. Some, like Andrés Castro and Juan Blanco, who proposed the crop cooperative, were heirless. Others had been less embroiled in the world of *amos* to begin with; they had industrialized production on their estates first and most fully, and they were already responsible for much of the village's agricultural work through rental arrangements, which they were finding increasingly problematic. Young men in general were more favorably disposed toward the proposals, since their involvement in the world of *amos*, peasants, and *casas* was slightest. The most ambivalent were the older small landowners. The long-term prospects that their *casas* would survive were dimmest, and they had already given up all but a semblance of control over their *casas'* agricultural production. Yet their identities were most bound to the *casa* as an autonomous realm of work and meaning.

As villagers remade Ibieca during the 1950s and 1960s, they did not erase the past. Nor did "cultural lag" lead them to attach meaning to their *casas*, to divisions between rich and poor, and to administrative issues in the cooperative debates. Rather, in the 1970s the past was still present in the village. The suspicions, tension, disavowals, and distancing that surfaced in discourse were the fruits of decades of witnessing each other's lives, of countless interactions, and of the continuous collective interpretive process known as gossip. Such a history is not shed like a snakeskin; it is the social body of the village. Juan Solano had watched his neighbors expropriate his father's estate and threaten his family during the Civil War. Villagers had witnessed Luis Solano expropriate collective crops and common land, had lived with the threat of his denunciation hanging over their heads for years, and had watched Juan assume similar liberties as he grew up. The division between Casa Solano and some of the smaller landholding *casas* was an especially intense one, but many other divisions between village *casas* festered until some incident or issue reopened them. These sores mattered to villagers, and they should matter to us in our effort to understand them.

Are grudges, distrust, and *casa* identities obstacles to cooperative formation? No; they are the idioms with which villagers understand their divisions, their inability to act collectively or effectively. There are also other idioms, of unity and cooperation, which villagers appeal to in order to account for their successful collective ventures. The idioms, like the events which determine which ones prevail, are the outcome of structured but open-ended historical experience. Neither the old nor the new social relations of agricultural production in Ibieca prohibit or compel cooperative formation. An agrarian cooperative represents a radical adaptation of the productive strategies of village *casas* and of political relations between them, but it is not one beyond the reach of village men, and they know it. Few are inclined to set up a cooperative themselves, and many are skeptical of others' proposals. But if a cooperative was forming, most would seriously consider joining it.

Alongside their memories of divisions and distrust were recollected connections and cooperations. Through ancient arrangements the village's families pastured their sheep in one flock, and they shared one *fuente*, one source of water, for themselves, their livestock, and their gardens. They may recall collective baking, a collective olive oil mill, labor- and machine-sharing. Many families still joined forces to slaughter and dress a pig each year. Productive ties, though weaker, still linked village families, as did the ties and festivities of kinship, marriage, and religious devotion. Twice a year village youths planned and carried off elaborate plays, games, and dances on Ibieca's major and minor feast days. For several years after Franco died, the young people sponsored Jornadas Culturales on the history, culture, economy, and politics of the Somontano and Aragon. In 1980, with the village priest, they set up the cooperatively run bar, Club Foces. During the years when I was visiting Ibieca, I saw them collaborate to install a running water and sewage system, to buy a TV for village use, to purchase a collective grain scale, and to pave village roads.

Forming an agrarian cooperative depended, just as did all other collective ventures, on a coalition of farmers making it happen. In Esquedas, in the western Somontano, and in areas designated for general cooperative development by the state, government agents actively constructed such coalitions and took considerable initiative in expediting the process of cooperative formation. Officials in IRYDA (Institute of Agrarian Reform and Development) told me that the central Somontano was politically weak, that its elites had little power in the provincial government and could not wrest a designation for development from it even if they tried. The officials also told me that the central government had never targeted the province for cooperative development or plot concentration programs, so government resources to assist cooperative formation were generally scarce. Therefore, in the central Somontano, coalitions would have to form out of processes internal to the villages and they would have to draw on their own contacts and resources. In Torres de Montes, one of the few villages in the central Somontano which formed an agrarian cooperative in the late 1970s, the mobilizing coalition consisted of three large landowners and the village priest. The landowners all had entrepreneurial skills and connections that reached beyond the village and agriculture; one had extensive experience with a cooperative in the western Somontano; and the priest had a passion for accounting.

A comparable coalition may or may not form in Ibieca. If one does, and an agrarian cooperative is set up, it will be no less and no more mysterious than a coalition and cooperative not forming. The mystery lies not in values or circumstances, but in the social body of Ibieca as it is lived by villagers. At best, we can describe a people's capacity to act collectively by examining their culture and their political economy, in both local and larger contexts. We cannot, however, understand why they actually do or do not act within those parameters without examining their specific historical experience and concrete social relationships.

Did the memory of anarchist collectivization affect the village men's response to the capitalist agrarian cooperative proposals? Certainly memories of misdeeds fueled some distrust, but it is difficult to tell if the prior experience shaped the response in any larger terms. The men surely noted the vast differences between the two forms of agrarian reorganization. The richer and the poorer stand in opposite relation to each agrarian reorganization: the landless gained what the rich gave up in the collective, whereas the cooperatives proposed in Ibieca offered materially more to the rich than to the poor. The collective made everyone into a worker, paid each according to his needs, and appropriated the surplus. The cooperative would hire workers, free members from work, and redistribute the surplus to them. The collective organized production, distribution, and consumption; the cooperative would leave *casas* intact as autonomous entities of consumption. The collective turned the social order on its head, and the cooperatives would renovate it drastically, but not radically. This time they, as a village and as individuals, would have to choose the agrarian reorganization, whereas the anarchist collective was presented to them as a fait accompli by the war.

The anarchist collective and the capitalist cooperative resembled each other in one important way. Both encountered resistance from small landowners in Ibieca because of the experienced or anticipated loss of *casa* autonomy as a productive entity, and hence of social identity. The fact that some small landowners used the same phrases (for example, "We are not prepared") to criticize the cooperative proposals and the anarchist collective suggests that the proposals recalled the historical experience. In this context, the fact that people would *choose* the cooperatives was trivial; that choice did not seem like an exercise of autonomy to small landowners, but appeared to be a decision to give up many of their prerogatives as masters of their own lives.

The Conclusion demonstrates that both the anarchist collective and the capitalist agrarian cooperative were distinctly disadvantaged as forms of social change alongside the market-mediated agrarian reforms of the Franco period. The collective and the cooperative confronted villagers full force with the social consequences of their choices, leading them to object, demur, and hold back. The social consequences of indirect agrarian reforms under Franco were, however, quite obscure. Although the *casa* in fact lost much of its autonomy as a result of those reforms, villagers do not make the connection. Indeed, as they accepted the incentives to change that were presented by market and state, they experienced themselves as preserving and amplifying *casa* autonomy. Yet those very decisions ultimately diminished that autonomy and remade them and their way of life, all without discourse or discord.

❧ Conclusion
❧ Between the
❧ Invisible Hand
❧ and the Iron Fist

If villagers form a capitalist agrarian cooperative in Ibieca, they will convert the agriculture of the village into a common enterprise, but they will not put the village back together again. The world of multidimensional, socially redolent interdependencies sustained by earlier forms of agricultural production was unmade with the agrarian reorganization of the 1950s and 1960s. *Casas* and the village as a whole dissolved as relatively autonomous ecological entities and were integrated more thoroughly into regional, national, and international market cycles. They also dissolved as productive units bound by complex relations of kinship, exchange, and wage labor; furthermore, local webs of work and kinship were not being reproduced by younger villagers, who moved in wider circles of their own design. Parental, religious, and political authorities that once bound villagers to their *casas* and to the village shriveled over the decades. Younger villagers became captivated by more secular, urban-dominated, regional and national systems of authority and belief.

How did things fall apart? Historically, as a matter of facts, figures, and individual lives, we have seen how it happened in Ibieca. Yet there lingers a sense of mystery. The village roared into the twentieth century and collapsed upon arrival. We are all—villagers, state agents, and analysts—so convinced that the agrarian reform project was first and foremost one of economic progress, of increasing agricultural production and the well-being of villagers, that we are mystified by how much was lost along the way. Many analysts appeal to urban influences, usually via emigration, as an independent cause of the social and cultural losses. Some villagers suspect that the goods delivered by progress were tainted. Gabriel Abadía thought that too much money split villagers apart by enabling them to buy things they did not need, which made them arrogant. Mariano Castillo also worried about the misfortune of having too much, and he thought the character of youth would benefit greatly if each young person went hungry one year out of every six. Even state agents took the agrarian reforms at their economic face value; thus the Delegate of Agriculture in Huesca was simply exasperated when he calculated that not even the large estates in Ibieca could turn a decent profit. What was the sense of agrarian reform if it did not make agriculture profitable?

The common flaw in such suppositions is that they take the narrow economic pretensions of the agrarian reforms too literally to begin with. However much agrarian reforms are cloaked in a rhetoric of improving agricultural production and the well-being of rural peoples, and however much those who carry them out genuinely believe that this is their only intent, agrarian reforms are by their nature campaigns of conquest, sometimes bloody and other times bloodless, waged by states against their rural peoples. Based on a careful study of agrarian reform programs carried out by eight very different regimes over the last 2,500 years, Elias Tuma came to this conclusion: "Though the objectives of reforms are varied, the primary ones are usually political regardless of who initiates reform. The reformers use reform to win the support of specific groups, to create or restore political stability, to legitimize their own political positions, or to create what they consider to be democracy. The timing and extent of the reforms are determined more by political pressure than by genuine economic and social needs of the rural population. . . . In every single case, legitimization of the regime or of the total political structure was a primary objective of the reformers."[1] Agrarian reform programs, whether they target land distribution or just the actual conduct of agriculture, are Trojan horses. Each carries within it an army of social and political realignments in the countryside, between urban and rural elites and markets, and between rural subjects and the state.

During the early nineteenth century successive Spanish governments fought over the fate of feudal elites and their subject popula-

---

1. Tuma, *Twenty-six Centuries of Agrarian Reform*, p. 233.

tions. During the early twentieth century successive governments fought over the fate of *caciques* and peasants. The future of the countryside was a central subject of contention of the Spanish Civil War as it was fought out between Nationalists and Republican Loyalists and among the factions which declared their loyalty to the Republic. Although Franco's victory was initially a victory for *caciques* and conservative peasants, within ten years political crisis and the strings attached to U.S. aid forced his regime to begin its slow and relentless about face in the countryside. Within two more decades Franco's agrarian reforms destroyed the productive bases of both *caciques* and peasants.

Franco's agrarian reforms simultaneously secured the food supply of growing cities, supplied industrial manufacturers with cheap labor and fresh consumer markets, and concentrated economic and political power in the central state. The directors of modern nation-states, now including Spain, have their hands on controls that can wipe out and redefine social worlds within their boundaries. With very slight adjustments—in prices, credit terms, pensions, quotas—the state can alter the panorama of production and the quality of life in the countryside. The future of farmers in Ibieca hangs primarily on the state price of cereals, on its movement in relation to soaring costs of production, and on state cooperative policies and programs. In 1979 an agrarian cooperative was barely within the reach of village farmers, and they were watching closely to see whether the state would move a cooperative further into or out of the realm of possibility. Agrarian and municipal reforms under Franco, and the radical reorganization of the political arena after Franco's death, finished off caciqual politics. Both peasants and *caciques* were marginal, relatively autonomous political creatures—not exactly outside the state, but not in it, either. Their conversion into farmers, workers, and pensioners robbed them of local power domains and placed them more squarely within the state, subject to its authority and its definition of politics.

The Franco regime, as it committed itself to capitalist industrialization and modern nation-state formation, committed itself to unmaking *caciques*, peasants, and their ways of life. Ibieca's story cannot shed any direct light on how the Franco regime came to those commitments, but we can draw from it some understanding of how that regime accomplished so radical a transformation in the countryside without provoking visible violence, or even concerted reaction. Elsewhere rural peoples have actively resisted the encroachment of state and market, and there was much organized contention over the fate of the countryside before Franco secured control of the state. All the reform efforts studied by Elias Tuma mobilized reactions, and in some quarters of Spain there was at least passive resistance to some of the explicit reform programs under Franco. Yet in the Somontano the very peasants and *caciques* who were unmade by the reform process continued to be among Franco's firmest supporters. The answer to why Franco's reform was politically successful lies between the Iron Fist and the Invisible Hand. That combination was also responsible for the mad-hatter quality of the reform process in Ibieca—the inescapable sense that things were never what they seemed, that they had quite unexpected and unintended consequences.

Direct agrarian reform efforts, such as land redistribution, involve intervention by state agencies in local communities; they are overt attempts to remake the conduct of agriculture or its social organization. Who will gain what, and who will lose what? The answers are generally clear. Both the Republican and anarchist reform efforts of the 1930s, for example, directly attacked the rural class structure. The Republican attack was weak in several respects but nevertheless proposed to redistribute large estates to the poor and landless. The anarchist collectivization during the Civil War did just that and more, as it abolished private productive property altogether. Such reforms either require explicit force, or they are resisted by those who stand to lose or who do not appreciate the gains. Agrarian reform programs that do not attack the class structure but still involve active state intervention and attempt to alter social relations and the organization of agricultural work also often produce active or passive resistance. The losses are plain, the gains are hypothetical, and there is a felt sense of "imposition" due to state involvement—a sense that autonomy will be lost in the process.

Indirect agrarian reforms do not, by definition, involve direct state intervention in local communities; instead, through them the state alters the conditions under which agriculture is organized and conducted. Some indirect reforms (for example, subsidies) clearly involve state agencies, but state agents do not go to villages and lobby for them. Most indirect reforms translate into market-mediated incentives. Either the state manipulates private markets (as in price and wage controls), or it expropriates a market (as in the case of wheat under Franco). Neither state subsidies nor market incentives engender a sense of "imposition" because the state's profile is low and because they both engage villagers in taking initiative to secure the incentives.

Indeed, villagers in Ibieca experienced the measures not as agrarian reforms aimed at altering their agricultural practice, but as business as usual via markets and a patronage state. Early reform measures during the 1950s were sufficiently corrupted or glossed as propaganda that their reforming effects seemed completely accidental. When they arrived in the province for rental to landowners, the COSA tractors appeared not as harbingers of a new world but as propaganda for Franco; and the Ministry of Agriculture tractors were sold at cut rates to "friends," *amos* with contacts in the Ministry, who resold them illegally to other *amos* at much higher prices. Gas and oil subsidies were notoriously abused until they were abolished in the 1970s. More market-mediated reforms, such as guaranteed prices, guaranteed purchase of wheat, and easy agrarian credit were not corrupted, or not corrupted so thoroughly, but the market itself served to obscure the reform agenda. During the 1960s the state relied increasingly on market manipulations, so that most village youth were only vaguely aware of the state's role in remaking Ibieca. When I asked them why the village had changed so much in their parents' lifetime, they replied, "Progress."

The agrarian reform under Franco did not arrive in the Somontano as a coherent package, nor did it explicitly claim to remake village ways. The reforms appeared as remotely connected "incentives" lodged in state agencies and market conditions, or as accents on already existing conditions that pertained to discrete practices, sales, or purchases. Who would have guessed that minute decisions to buy, sell, borrow, and rent would change so much so quickly?

Here is the real secret of the Invisible Hand's power to remake social relations: the discrepancy, the chasm, between the individual decisionmaking process it engages and the collective consequences it engenders. Individual villagers decided to rent tractors one year in the early 1950s, then again the next year, and the next. A few, quite independently, bought tractors; others, independently again, decided to rent them. As costs and prices moved against grapes and olives and in favor of wheat, villagers decided to shift more land into wheat; when the ratio favored barley over wheat, they shifted again. Who would have guessed that, in making these individual, independent decisions, they were altering the ecology and social relations of village agricultural production, and hence of their way of life? The mystery, the eeriness, is compounded when we recall that villagers made decisions such as these so that their *casas* might survive and prosper as ever—not so that they would become something different. The social and ecological meaning of buying into consumer markets was equally obscure. Independent decisions to buy clothes, cars, factory furniture, toilets, stoves, washing machines, bread, olive oil, wine, meat, and vegetables chipped away at local cycles and social connections until they were all but destroyed. We cannot begrudge villagers these things, much less their better access to education, health care, and pensions. But who could have guessed that so much culture and community would be snatched away in the process?

None of the incentives to which villagers responded came with their social implications spelled out. Over time the village changed visibly, in its practices and its possessions. It also changed invisibly—even the meanings of things that stayed the same changed. What it meant to be a *casa* heir or non-heir, to be young or old, to be a man or a woman, was eaten away and reconstructed from within. At some point in the lives of most village elders, the familiar became strange, and somehow they were accomplices in their own estrangement. The reformation was not imposed by force; as individuals, they could hold out for some time against the changing market conditions, or they could emigate—all of which lent an aura of choice to those who actively reformed agriculture in Ibieca. Thus the elders were implicated in the larger process of remaking Ibieca, in the very process that converted the motives and values behind their choices into irrelevant antiques. Another secret of the Invisible Hand: it implicates individuals in the unforeseen collective consequences of their decisions because those decisions are experienced as voluntary choices.

No one came to Ibieca and told villagers to change or be eliminated. At the same time, under Franco's Iron Fist, villagers had no access to political processes by which they might have arrived at a shared consciousness of, or willingness to contend about, the collective implications of the decisions. The agrarian reform was not imposed physically, but it was imposed in the sense that villagers ultimately had no choice but to accept it. It was also imposed by its hiddenness, its disguise as the Invisible Hand which at once obscured social consequences and created a powerful illusion that one brought one's world entirely upon oneself. A dictatorship that effectively turns capitalism into its agent, and hence itself into capitalism's agent, is culturally most virulent.

Villagers were perfectly free to keep plowing with their mules. Meanwhile, wages, prices, and credit terms shifted, creating incentives for mechanized methods that simultaneously served as disincentives for old methods. Gradually the cost of mules and tools rose. Eventually it became costlier to use old methods than new ones. Finally, in the early 1970s, it was hard to find a young, strong mule for sale in the province of Huesca, and *amos* and peasants were no longer so free to keep plowing with mules. Wage, price, and credit movements had unobtrusively and mysteriously withdrawn old forms of production and deposited new ones. The processes that defined alternatives and ways of life in and out of existence seemed so remote and abstract that it was difficult to focus a sense of injustice and outrage on a perpetrating source. Villagers either accepted the changing conditions, joined with the trends they engendered, and identified with them; or they held out and were isolated, quietly derided, and forgotten. There was no ugly process of elimination; just a slow, clean, cultural death.

Appendix

1. Population of Ibieca, 1495–1975

Year	Population
1495	75
1565	60
1646	105
1717	150
1838	324
1857	398
1877	389
1887	443
1900	401
1910	392
1920	355
1930	301
1940	298
1950	284
1960	240
1970	167
1975	150

Sources: Biblioteca Nacional de España, "Investigación de los fuegos" and "Relación de 1717"; Archivo de la Real Academia, "Registro de año 1646"; Durán Guidol, *Geographía Medieval*; Diputación Provincial de Huesca, "Relación de las almas"; Instituto Geográfico y Estadístico, *Censo de 1857, Censo de 1877, Censo de 1887*; Instituto Nacional de Estadística, *Censo de 1960*, village census records.

2. Area of Land per Crop in Ibieca, 1860–1974 (in Hectares)

	1860	1945	1956	1969	1974
Cereals			259	370	606
Fallow			160	220	95
Total Fallow and Cereals	565	534	419	590	701
Vines	204	61	59	20	20
Olives	31	82	94	92	75
Almonds		17	47	60	50
Total Orchard and Vineyard	235	160	200	172	145
Gardens and Forage Crops	9	7	5	11	50
Total Cultivated	809	701	624	863	896
Total Uncultivated	611	710	796	732	574
Total Cultivated and Uncultivated	1420	1411	1420	1595	1470

Sources: Ministerio de Hacienda de Huesca, "Cadastro de Ibieca" for 1860, 1945, and 1956; village records for 1969; Diputación Provincial de Huesca, *Estudio Socioeconómico* for 1974.

3. Day Laborer Wages and Cost of Living in Ibieca, 1940–73

Year	Daily Wage (pesetas)	Cost of Living Index
1940	3	17
1950	10	36
1953	15	39
1955	25	41
1960	74	59
1963	100	69
1973	250	108

Sources: These wages were reported to me by villagers. Cost-of-living figures are from unpublished tables for Huesca capital from the Instituto Nacional de Estadística in Huesca.

4. Land Distribution in Aragon, 1962–72

Size of Estate	1962		1972	
	% of Land-owners	% of Land Owned	% of Land-owners	% of Land Owned
0–10 Hectares	67	7.5	58.5	6.5
10–100 Hectares	30	29	37	29
Over 100 Hectares	3	63.5	4.5	64

Source: Biescas, *Introducción a la economía de la región aragonesa*, p. 112.

Bibliography

Aceves, Joseph. *Social Change in a Spanish Village*. Cambridge: Schenkman, 1971.

———, and Douglass, William, eds. *The Changing Faces of Rural Spain*. Cambridge: Schenkman, 1976.

Anderson, Charles W. *The Political Economy of Spain*. Madison: University of Wisconsin Press, 1970.

Archivo de la Real Academia de la Historia. "Registro del vecindario del reyno de Aragón de año 1646." Colección Nasarre. Madrid (1646).

Aya, Roderick. *The Missed Revolution: The Fate of Rural Rebels in Sicily and Southern Spain, 1840-1950*. Papers on European and Mediterranean Societies, no. 3. Amsterdam: University of Amsterdam Anthropological-Sociological Centre, 1975.

Aznar Navarro, Francisco. "Los señores aragoneses: actos de posesión y homenajes." *Cultura Española* 4 (1907):930–40.

Banfield, E. C. *The Moral Basis of a Backward Society*. New York: Free Press, 1958.

Barrett, Richard A. "Social Hierarchy and Intimacy in a Spanish Town." *Ethnology* 11, no. 4 (1972):386–98.

———. *Benabarre: The Modernization of a Spanish Village*. New York: Holt, Rinehart and Winston, 1974.

Benjamin, Walter. *Illuminations*. New York: Harcourt, Brace and World, 1968.

Berger, John. *Pig Earth*. New York: Pantheon, 1979.

Berkner, L. K. "The Stem Family and the Developmental Cycle of the Peasant Household: An Eighteenth-Century Austrian Example." *American Historical Review* 77 (1972):398–418.

Biblioteca Nacional de España. "Investigación de los fuegos que ay en los ceudades, villas y lugares del reyno de Aragón que se hizo el año MCCCCXCV." MS. 746. Madrid (1495).

———. "Relación del vecindario del reyno de Aragón sobre repartición de la contribución que se mando exigir este corriente año de 1717." MS. 2,274. Madrid (1717).

Biescas, J. Antonio. *Introducción a la economía de la región aragonesa*. Zaragoza: Alcrudo Editor, 1977.

Blok, Anton. *The Mafia of a Sicilian Village*. New York: Harper, 1974.

Bolloten, Burnett. *The Grand Camouflage*. New York: Frederick A. Praeger, 1961.

Bookchin, Murray. *The Spanish Anarchists: The Heroic Years, 1868-1936*. New York: Harper, 1977.

Borkenau, Franz. *The Spanish Cockpit*. Ann Arbor: University of Michigan Press, 1963.

Brandes, Stanley H. *Migration, Kinship and Community: Tradition and Transition in a Spanish Village.* New York: Academic Press, 1975.

Brenan, Gerald. *The Face of Spain.* London: Penguin, 1950.

———. *The Spanish Labyrinth.* Cambridge: Cambridge University Press, 1967.

Caja Rural Provincial. *Memoría, ejercicio de 1975.* Huesca: Octavio y Felez, 1976.

Carr, Raymond. *Spain, 1808-1939.* Oxford: Oxford University Press, 1966.

Casas Torres, José. "Los hombres y en trabajo." *Aragón.* 2 vols., ed. José Casas Torres. Zaragoza: Banco de Aragón, 1960.

Chayanov, A. V. *The Theory of Peasant Economy.* Homewood, Ill.: Richard D. Irwin, 1966.

Chomsky, Noam. "Objectivity and Liberal Scholarship." In *American Power and the New Mandarins.* New York: Vintage, 1969.

Christian, William A., Jr. *Person and God in a Spanish Valley.* New York: Seminar Press, 1972.

Cole, John W. "Anthropology Comes Part-Way Home: Community Studies in Europe." *Annual Review of Anthropology* 6 (1977).

———, and Wolf, Eric R. *The Hidden Frontier: Ecology and Ethnicity in an Alpine Valley.* New York: Academic, 1974.

Consejo Económico Sindical Provincial de Huesca. *Ponencias y conclusiones del IV pleno del consejo económico sindical provincial de Huesca.* Madrid: R. García Blanco, 1967.

Daumas, Max. *La Vie rurale dans le haut Aragon oriental.* Madrid: Consejo Superior de Investigaciones Científicas, 1976.

del Arco, Ricardo. *Nuevas pinturas murales en la iglesia de San Miguel de Foces, monumento nacional.* Madrid: Tipografía de Archivos, 1932.

Diario de Huesca, vols. 18, 21, 26, 1892-1900.

Diputación Provincial de Huesca. "Relación de las almas de los pueblos de la provincia de Huesca." *Boletín oficial del govierno político de Huesca.* April, 1838.

———, and Economistas Asociados. *Estudio socioeconómico de la provincia de Huesca, muncipio de Ibieca.* Zaragoza: Economistas Asociados, 1976.

Domínguez Ortiz, Antonio. *La Sociedad española en el siglo XVIII.* Madrid: Consejo Superior de Investigaciones Científicas, 1955.

Douglass, William A. *Echalar and Murelaga: Opportunity and Rural Exodus in Two Basque Villages.* New York: St. Martin's Press, 1975.

Durán Guidol, Antonio. *Geografía medieval de los obispados de jaca y Huesca.* Huesca: Argensola, 1961.

Erikson, Kai T. *Everything in Its Path: Destruction of Community in the Buffalo Creek Flood.* New York: Simon and Schuster, 1976.

Esteva Fabregat, Claudio. "Para una teoría de la aculturación en el alto Aragón." *Ethnica* 2 (1971).

Fernández Clemente, Eloy. *Aragón contemporaneo, 1833-1936.* Madrid: Siglo XXI de España Editores, 1975.

Franklin, S. H. *The European Peasantry: The Final Phase.* London: Methuen, 1969.

Fraser, Ronald. *In Hiding: The Life of Manuel Cortes.* New York: Pantheon, 1972.

_____. "1936: Revolutionary Committees in Spain." *New Left Review* 78 (March-April 1973).

_____. *Tajos: The Story of a Village on the Costa del Sol.* New York: Pantheon, 1973.

_____. *Blood of Spain: An Oral History of the Spanish Civil War.* New York: Pantheon, 1979.

Freeman, Susan Tax. *Neighbors.* Chicago: University of Chicago Press, 1970.

Friedman, Harriet. "World Market and International Trade: The Case of Wheat, 1873-1935." Paper presented at the International Studies Association, 1977. Mimeo.

García Delagado, José Luis, ed. *La Cuestión agraria en la España contemporanea.* Madrid: Cuadernos para el Dialogo, 1976.

García-Pelayo, Manuel. *Las Transformaciones del estado contemporaneo.* Madrid: Alianza Editorial, 1977.

Gilmore, David. "Land Reform and Rural Revolt in Nineteenth-Century Andalusia (Spain)." *Peasant Studies* 6, no. 4 (October 1977).

_____. "Carnaval in Fuenmayor: Class Conflict and Social Cohesion in an Andalusian Town." *Journal of Anthropological Research* 31, no. 4 (Winter 1975).

_____ *The People of the Plain.* New York: Columbia University Press, 1980.

Gómez Mendoza, Josefina. *Agricultura y expansión urbana.* Madrid: Alianza Editorial, 1977.

Greenwood, Davydd. *Unrewarding Wealth: The Commercialization and Collapse of Agriculture in a Spanish Basque Town.* Cambridge: Cambridge University Press, 1976.

Hansen, Edward C. *Rural Catalonia under the Franco Regime: The Fate of Regional Culture since the Spanish Civil War.* Cambridge: Cambridge University Press, 1977.

Harding, Susan. "Women and Words in a Spanish Village." In *Toward an Anthropology of Women,* ed. Rayna R. Reiter. New York: Monthly Review Press, 1975.

_____. "Agrarian Reform Disguised as the Invisible Hand in Franco Spain." *Peasant Studies* 5, no. 3 (July 1976).

_____. "Street Shouting and Shunning: Conflict between Women in a Spanish Village." *Frontiers* 3, no. 3 (1978).

Herr, Richard. *The Eighteenth-Century Revolution in Spain.* Princeton: Princeton University Press, 1958.

_____. *Spain.* Englewood Cliffs, N.J.: Prentice-Hall, 1971.

Hobsbawm, E. J. *Primitive Rebels: Studies in Archaic Forms of Social*

Movements in the 19th and 20th Centuries. New York: W. W. Norton, 1965.

Instituto Geográfico y Estadístico. *Censo de la población de España, 1857.* Madrid: IGE, 1858.

_____. *Censo de la población de España, 1877.* Madrid: IGE, 1883-84.

_____. *Censo de la población de España, 1887.* Madrid: IGE, 1891-92.

_____. *Censo de la población de España, 1897.* Madrid: IGE, 1899.

Instituto Nacional de Estadística. *Reseña estadística de la provincia de Huesca.* Madrid: INE, 1955.

_____. *Censo de la población de las viviendas de España, 1960.* Vol. 1. Madrid: INE, 1962.

_____. *Primer censo agrario de España, Octubre de 1962: Huesca.* No. 22. Madrid: INE Artes Graficas, 1964.

_____. *Reseña estadística de la provincia de Huesca.* Madrid: Soc. de Rivadeneyra, 1970.

_____. *Censo agrario de España, 1972: Huesca.* No. 22. Madrid: INE Artes Graficas, 1973.

_____. *Censo de la población de España de 1970.* Vols. 4–22. Madrid: Imprenta Nacional del Boletín Oficial del Estado, 1973.

Jackson, Gabriel. *The Spanish Republic and the Civil War, 1931-1939.* Princeton: Princeton University Press, 1965.

_____. "The Living Experience of the Spanish Civil War Collectives." *Newsletter of the Society for Spanish and Portuguese Historical Studies* 1, no. 2 (April 1970).

Kaplan, Temma. *Anarchists of Andalusia, 1868-1903.* Princeton: Princeton University Press, 1977.

Kenny, Michael. "Patterns of Patronage in Spain." *Anthropological Quarterly* 33, no. 1 (1960).

_____. "Parallel Power Structures in Castile: The Patron-Client Balance." In *Contributions to Mediterranean Sociology,* ed. J. G. Peristiany. The Hague: Mouton, 1963.

_____. *A Spanish Tapestry: Town and Country in Castile.* New York: Harper, 1966.

Kern, Robert W. "Spanish Caciquismo, a Classic Model." In *The Caciques,* ed. Robert W. Kern. Albuquerque: University of New Mexico Press, 1973.

_____. *Liberals, Reformers, and Caciques in Restoration Spain, 1875-1909.* Albuquerque: University of New Mexico Press, 1974.

Ladurie, Emmanuel LeRoy. *Montaillou: The Promised Land of Error.* New York: Vintage, 1979.

Leal, José Luis, et al. *La Agricultura en el desarrollo capitalista español.* Madrid: Siglo XXI, 1975.

Linz, Juan J. "An Authoritarian Regime: Spain." In *Cleavages, Ideologies and Party Systems,* ed. Erik Allardt and Yrjö Littunen. Helsinki: Westermark Society, 1964.

Lisón-Tolosana, Carmelo. *Belmonte de los Caballeros.* Oxford: Clarendon Press, 1966.

López de Sebastián, José. *Política agraria en España, 1920-1970.* Madrid: Guardiana de Publicaciones, 1970.

Madoz, Pascual. *Diccionario geográfico-estadístico-histórico de España y sus posesiones de ultramar.* 16 vols. Madrid, 1847.

Malefakis, Edward. *Agrarian Reform and Peasant Revolution in Spain.* New Haven: Yale University Press, 1970.

_____. "Internal Political Problems and Loyalties: The Republican Side of the Spanish Civil War." In *Civil Wars in the Twentieth Century,* ed. Robin Higham. Lexington: University Press of Kentucky, 1972.

_____. "Peasants, Politics, and Civil War in Spain, 1931-1939." In *Modern European Social History,* ed. Robert Beucha. Lexington, Mass.: D.C. Heath, 1972.

Marti, Henri. "Agriculture and Politics in Spain, 1936-1960." Ph.D. dissertation, University of Michigan, 1979.

Martínez-Alier, Juan. *Labourers and Landowners in Southern Spain.* London: Allen and Unwin, 1971.

Martínez Cuadrado, Miguel. *La burguesía conservadors, 1874-1931.* Madrid: Alianza Universal, 1974.

Maurice, Jacques. *La Reforma agraria en España en el siglo XX, 1900-1936.* Madrid: Siglo XXI, 1975.

Merino y Hernández, José-Luis. *Aragón y su derecho.* Zaragoza: Guara Editorial, 1978.

Ministerio de Agricultura. *Coeficientes horarios para las operaciones del cultivo de cereales.* Madrid: Publicacions del Minsterio de Agricultura, 1968.

Ministerio de Estado. *Censo Español.* Madrid: Imprenta Real, 1787.

Ministerio de Hacienda de Huesca. "Cadastro de Ibieca." Huesca, 1860.

_____. "Cadastro de Ibieca." Huesca, 1945.

_____. "Cadastro de Ibieca." Huesca, 1956.

Mintz, Jerome R. *The Anarchists of Casas Viejas.* Chicago: University of Chicago Press, 1982.

Moore, Barrington, Jr. *Social Origins of Dictatorship and Democracy.* Boston: Beacon Press, 1966.

Nadal, Jordí. *La Población española (Siglos XVI a XX).* Barcelona: Ariel, 1973.

Naredo, José Manuel. *La Evolución de la agricultura en España.* Barcelona: Estela Editorial, 1971.

Navarro Tomás, Tomás. *Documentos lingüísticos del alto Aragón.* Syracuse, N.Y.: Syracuse University Press, 1957.

Orwell, George. *Homage to Catalonia.* Boston: Beacon Press, 1955.

Payne, Stanley, ed. *Politics and Society in Twentieth-Century Spain.* New York: New Viewpoints, 1976.

Peirats, José. *La CNT en la revolución española.* 3 vols. Paris: Ruedo Iberico, 1971.

Pérez-Díaz, Victor M. *Pueblos y clases sociales en el campo español.* Madrid: Siglo XXI, 1974.

Pitt-Rivers, Julian. *The People of the Sierra.* Chicago: University of Chicago Press, 1961.

Poggi, Gianfranco. *The Development of the Modern State.* Stanford: Stanford University Press, 1978.

Poulantzas, Nicos. *The Crisis of the Dictatorships.* London: New Left Books, 1976.

Pujadas, Juan José, and Comas, Dolores. "La 'casa' en el proceso de cambio del Pirineo Aragonés." *Cuadernos de investigación 2.* Logroño: Colegio Universitario de Logroño, 1975.

Reiter, Rayna R. "Men and Women in the South of France: Public and Private Domains." In her *Toward an Anthropology of Women.* New York: Monthly Review Press, 1975.

Sánchez Albornoz, Nicolas. *España hace un siglo: Una economía dual.* Madrid: Alianza, 1977.

Schneider, Jane, and Schneider, Peter. "Economic Dependence and the Failure of Cooperatives in Western Sicily." No. 1830. Chicago: Ninth International Congress of Anthropological and Ethnological Sciences, 1972.

————. *Culture and Political Economy in Western Sicily.* New York: Academic Press, 1976.

Schneider, Peter; Schneider, Jane; and Hansen, Edward C. "Modernization and Development: The Role of Regional Elites and Non-Corporate Groups in the European Mediterranean." *Comparative Studies in Society and History* 14 (1972).

Sevilla-Guzmán, Eduardo. *La Evolución del campesianado en España.* Barcelona: Ediciones Peninsula, 1979.

Silverman, Sydel. "Agricultural Organization, Social Structure, and Values in Italy: Amoral Familism Reconsidered." *American Anthropologist* 70 (1968).

————. *Three Bells of Civilization.* New York: Columbia University Press, 1975.

Simón Segura, Francisco. *La Desamortización española del siglo XIX.* Madrid: Instituto de Estudios Fiscales, 1973.

Souchy, Agustín. *Entre los campesinos de Aragón.* Barcelona: Ediciones Tierra y Libertad, 1937.

Swartz, Marc, ed. *Local Level Politics.* Chicago: Aldine, 1969.

Tamames, Ramón. *Estructura económica de España.* Madrid: Guardiana de Publicaciones, 1971.

————. *La República, la era de Franco.* Madrid: Alianza Universal, 1973.

Thomas, Hugh. "Anarchist Agrarian Collectives in the Spanish Civil War." In *A Century of Conflict, 1850-1950,* ed. Martin Gilbert. New York: Atheneum, 1967.

Tilly, Charles. "Rural Collective Action in Modern Europe." In *Forging Nations: A Comparative View of Rural Ferment and Revolt,* eds. Joseph Spielberg and Scott Whiteford. East Lansing: Michigan State University Press, 1976.

_____. *The Formation of National States in Western Europe.* Princeton: Princeton University Press, 1975.

Tipps, Dean C. "Modernization Theory and the Comparative Study of Societies: A Cultural Perspective." *Comparative Studies in Society and History* 15, no. 2 (March 1973).

Tuma, Elias. *Twenty-six Centuries of Agrarian Reform, A Comparative Analysis.* Berkeley: University of California Press, 1965.

Tussell Gómez, Xavier. "The Functioning of the Cacique System in Andalusia, 1890-1931." In *Politics and Society in Twentiety-Century Spain,* ed. Stanley Payne. New York: New Viewpoints, 1976.

_____. *La Reforma de la administración local en España.* Madrid: Instituto de Estudios Administrativos, 1973.

United States. Department of State. *Foreign Relations of the United States, 1949.* Vol. 4: Western Europe. Washington: U.S. Government Printing Office, 1975.

Urquijo, Alfonso de, and Biarge López, Aurelio. *Alto Aragón, su historia y arte.* Seville: Imprenta Sevillana, 1977.

Vicens Vives, J. *Manual de historia económica de España.* Vol. 1. Barcelona: Editorial Teide, 1959.

Wallerstein, Immanuel. *The Modern World-System: Capitalist Agriculture and the Origins of the European World-Economy in the Sixteenth Century.* New York: Academic Press, 1974.

Wolf, Eric. *Peasant Wars of the Twentieth Century.* New York: Harper and Row, 1969.

Index